ROTISSERIE OVEN COOKING

Sandra Rudloff

BRISTOL PUBLISHING ENTERPRISES
San Leandro, California

A **nitty gritty**® Cookbook

©2001 Bristol Publishing Enterprises, Inc., P.O. Box 1737, San Leandro, California 94577. World rights reserved. No part of this publication may be reproduced in any form, nor may it be stored in a retrieval system, transmitted, or otherwise copied for public or private use without prior written permission from the publisher.

Printed in the United States of America.

ISBN: 1-55867-267-2

Cover design: Frank J. Paredes
Cover photography: John A. Benson
Food stylist: Susan Devaty
Illustrations: Grant Corley

CONTENTS

- **1**   Rotisserie Oven Cooking
- **3**   Rubs and Marinades
- **29**   Steaks, Chops, Kabobs and More
- **58**   Large Cuts of Meat
- **71**   Whole Poultry
- **90**   Seafood
- **118**   Rotisserie Vegetables and Fruits
- **151**   Index

ROTISSERIE OVEN COOKING

We've all seen them in restaurants and markets: those multi-tiered rotisseries busy cooking roasts and chickens. Why is rotisserie food so popular? Because no other cooking method offers you such even cooking and constant basting. The juices that would normally end up on the bottom of a pan are constantly basting your meat.

Until recently, the only way for home cooks to utilize rotisserie cooking was the barbecue. But thanks to new countertop rotisserie ovens, anyone can use a rotisserie, at any time of year.

Poultry really benefits from rotisserie cooking, as the juices from the meat do not settle at the bottom of the bird, as they do when roasting traditionally. With rotisserie cooking, the breast meat is as tender and juicy as the dark meat.

Rotisserie cooking is not limited to large cuts of meat or poultry. Many rotisserie ovens come with multiple attachments for smaller cuts of meat and even fish and vegetables.

The cooking times in this book are approximate: your oven may have temperature control settings and multiple heating elements, while many other brands of rotisserie don't have those features. Please refer to your owner's manual for cooking time estimates.

Instant-read thermometers should be used when cooking in a rotisserie oven. Until you get to know your oven, they are the easiest and best way to check for doneness. You don't need to take the food out to check; just stop the rotisserie bar from turning (by pausing or stopping the motor), check and then start up the motor again.

RUBS AND MARINADES

- **5** About Using Dried Rubs and Marinades
- **6** Herbes de Provence
- **7** Old Bay Rub for Seafood
- **8** Creole Rub
- **9** Italian Beef Rub
- **10** Herb Rub for Lamb
- **11** Jamaican Jerk Rub for Pork or Poultry
- **12** Sage Rub for Lamb or Poultry
- **13** Ranch Rub for Beef
- **14** Baja Marinade for Seafood
- **15** Herb Marinade for Seafood
- **16** Marinade for Seafood
- **17** Tarragon Marinade for Seafood
- **18** Citrus Marinade for Seafood

19	Dijon Marinade for Poultry and Seafood
20	Fresh Herb Marinade for Poultry
21	White Wine Marinade for Poultry
22	Italian Marinade for Poultry
23	Mint Marinade for Lamb
24	Marinade for Pork
25	Orange Ginger Marinade for Pork or Poultry
26	Red Wine Marinade for Beef
27	Tuscan Beef Marinade
28	Whisky Marinade for Ribs

ABOUT USING DRIED RUBS AND MARINADES

This section contains dry rubs and marinades for meats, poultry and seafood. They can be used on any cut or size of meat; be sure to increase quantities as needed.

When marinating meats and poultry, always marinate for a minimum of 30 minutes at room temperature, or up to 24 hours in the refrigerator. Do not keep your meats or poultry at room temperature for more than 30 minutes before cooking. Seafood tends to absorb marinades faster, so marinating seafood for more than 30 minutes is not recommended. Also, if the seafood marinade contains vinegar, wine or citrus juices, the seafood texture will change to a "cooked" texture, which will affect the final cooked version (the seafood dish seviche is raw fish that has been marinated in citrus juices; even though the fish is raw, it has a "cooked," firm texture and is opaque in color).

Rubs work best when allowed to stay on the meats for a period of time before cooking. This allows the meat's juices to absorb the flavors, and for the rubs to adhere better. One big benefit of using the rotisserie for cooking when using rubs is that your rub won't stick to the grill or pan, but stays on your food.

Most poultry marinades and rubs can be used on pork or seafood. Seafood marinades and rubs can be used on poultry also, but not usually other meats. All of the recipes in this section are quick ways to add flavor to your rotisseried entrée.

HERBES DE PROVENCE

This classic blend of herbs gives a French flavor to poultry, meats and seafood. This makes about 1½ cups of herbs, so store what you don't use in an airtight container.

¼ cup dried rosemary
¼ cup dried thyme
¼ cup dried basil
¼ cup dried oregano
¼ cup dried marjoram
¼ cup dried savory
1 tsp. freshly ground black pepper

Combine all ingredients in a small bowl. Use as a dry rub on meats, poultry, fish and lamb.

OLD BAY RUB FOR SEAFOOD

This is a good rub for firm-fleshed fish steaks, such as halibut, tuna, mahi-mahi and cod.

1 tbs. Old Bay seasoning
2 tbs. minced fresh parsley
1 clove garlic, minced
grated zest of 1 lemon

Combine all ingredients in a glass or ceramic dish. Gently press into fish. Let stand for 30 minutes before cooking.

CREOLE RUB

The same herbs used for "blackening" are adjusted and used as a rub in this recipe. You'll get a deep, complex Creole flavor on your meats. This rub can also be used on seafood and gives especially good results with chicken.

2 tbs. brown sugar, packed
2 tbs. paprika
1 tbs. freshly ground black pepper
2 tsp. cayenne pepper
2 tsp. garlic salt
1 tsp. celery salt

Combine all ingredients in a small bowl. Sprinkle on all surfaces of meat, poultry, pork or seafood and press in lightly. Let stand for 1 hour before cooking.

ITALIAN BEEF RUB

Most people wouldn't associate Italian flavors with a meat rub. My favorite use for this rub is on thickly cut steaks.

1 tsp. dried basil
1 tsp. dried oregano
1 tsp. dried rosemary, broken into tiny pieces
½ tsp. garlic salt
½ tsp. freshly ground pepper

Combine all ingredients in a small bowl. Sprinkle on all surfaces of beef and press in lightly. Let stand for 1 hour before cooking.

HERB RUB FOR LAMB

Along with mint, rosemary is a frequent partner for lamb. Triple the ingredients and you will have enough for a leg of lamb.

1 tbs. minced fresh rosemary
2 tsp. minced fresh thyme leaves
1 clove garlic, minced
½ tsp. salt
grated zest of 1 lemon

Combine all ingredients in a glass or ceramic dish. Press into lamb lightly. Let stand for 1 hour before cooking.

JAMAICAN JERK RUB FOR PORK OR POULTRY

You can use commercial jerk sauce for the spicy Caribbean dish known as "jerk," but this rub will give you the same intense flavors. Try this rub on pork spareribs—it makes a great appetizer if you cut the ribs into small sections before cooking.

1 tsp. garlic powder
1 tsp. onion powder
2 tbs. ground allspice
2 tbs. brown sugar, packed
4 tsp. cinnamon
1 tsp. nutmeg
1 tsp. cayenne pepper

Combine all ingredients in a small bowl. Sprinkle on all surfaces of pork or poultry and press in lightly. Let stand for 1 hour before cooking.

SAGE RUB FOR LAMB OR POULTRY

Traditional poultry seasonings are combined to create this rub. When used on poultry, you'll have the taste of an old-fashioned meal.

1 tbs. ground sage
1 tsp. garlic powder
2 tsp. dried rosemary, crushed
1 tsp. ground thyme
½ tsp. salt
½ tsp. freshly ground black pepper

Combine all ingredients in a small bowl. Sprinkle on all surfaces of lamb or poultry and press in lightly. Let stand for 1 hour before cooking.

RANCH RUB FOR BEEF

This is the simplest way to season good cuts of beef—the flavors are mild and complement the beef without overpowering it. This is a good rub for steaks.

1 tbs. freshly ground black pepper
1 tbs. onion powder
1 tbs. garlic powder
1 tsp. salt

Combine all ingredients in a small bowl. Sprinkle on all surfaces of beef and press in lightly. Let stand for 1 hour before cooking.

BAJA MARINADE FOR SEAFOOD

Lime, cilantro and hot pepper sauce make a zesty "Cal-Mex" marinade. Try this on prawns for a great appetizer.

¼ cup fresh lime juice
grated zest of 1 lime
½ cup white wine
¼ cup vegetable oil
½ cup chopped fresh cilantro
1 clove garlic, minced
1 tbs. Tabasco Sauce or other hot pepper sauce

Combine all ingredients in a glass or ceramic dish. Add seafood and marinate for 30 minutes at room temperature, turning occasionally. Discard remaining marinade.

HERB MARINADE FOR SEAFOOD

The herb mixture in this marinade might be a bit strong for delicate fish; try this using firm and meaty steaks such as tuna, shark or swordfish.

1/4 cup olive oil
2 tbs. chopped fresh parsley
2 tbs. dried thyme
1 tbs. dried rosemary
1 clove garlic, minced
1/2 tsp. salt
2 tbs. freshly squeezed lemon juice

Combine all ingredients in a glass or ceramic dish. Add seafood and marinate for 30 minutes at room temperature. Discard remaining marinade.

MARINADE FOR SEAFOOD

If you don't want strong flavors on your seafood, this marinade is the one to choose. It adds a slight lemon and herb taste to most seafood and shellfish.

1/4 cup fresh lemon juice
1 cup white wine
1 tbs. dried tarragon
2 tsp. dried dill
1/2 tsp. black pepper

Combine all ingredients in a glass or ceramic dish. Add seafood and marinate for 30 minutes at room temperature, turning occasionally. Discard remaining marinade.

TARRAGON MARINADE FOR SEAFOOD

If you love the taste of tarragon tuna salad, try this marinade on tuna steaks. It is also great on red snapper fillets.

¼ cup olive oil
2 cloves garlic, minced
¾ tsp. dried tarragon
½ tsp. salt

Combine all ingredients in a glass or ceramic dish. Add seafood and marinate for 30 minutes at room temperature. Discard remaining marinade.

CITRUS MARINADE FOR SEAFOOD

The sweet flavors of this Hawaiian-inspired marinade work best with mild fish such as halibut or sole.

½ cup freshly squeezed orange juice
¼ cup freshly squeezed lemon juice
¼ cup pineapple juice
¼ cup vegetable oil
½ tsp. ground ginger

Combine all ingredients in a glass or ceramic dish. Add seafood and marinate for 30 minutes at room temperature. Discard remaining marinade.

DIJON MARINADE FOR POULTRY AND SEAFOOD

White wine and Dijon mustard are a classic French pairing. Together they will give your poultry and seafood a taste of "country French" cooking.

1 cup white wine
1/3 cup Dijon mustard
2 tbs. olive oil
1 tsp. dried tarragon
1/2 tsp. salt

Combine all ingredients in a glass or ceramic dish. Add poultry or seafood and marinate for 30 minutes at room temperature, or up to 8 hours in the refrigerator, turning occasionally. Discard remaining marinade.

FRESH HERB MARINADE FOR POULTRY

This simple herb marinade not only flavors your poultry, but the herbs cling to the skin or meat, making a pretty presentation when done.

½ cup white wine
½ cup olive oil
¼ cup red wine vinegar
2 cloves garlic, minced
2 tbs. minced fresh Italian parsley
2 tbs. minced fresh basil
2 tbs. minced fresh rosemary

Combine all ingredients in a glass or ceramic dish. Add poultry and marinate for 30 minutes at room temperature, or up to 8 hours in the refrigerator, turning occasionally. Discard remaining marinade.

WHITE WINE MARINADE FOR POULTRY

If you are in the mood for turkey, try this marinade on turkey pieces for a lighter meal than traditionally roasted turkey.

1 1/2 cups white wine
1 clove garlic, minced
1/4 tsp. freshly ground black pepper
1/2 tsp. dried thyme
1/2 tsp. dried sage

Combine all ingredients in a glass or ceramic dish. Add poultry and marinate for 30 minutes at room temperature, or up to 8 hours in the refrigerator, turning occasionally. Discard remaining marinade.

ITALIAN MARINADE FOR POULTRY

I like to use this marinade on chicken cut into pieces; cool and serve the cooked pieces for an Italian-inspired picnic.

1 1/2 cups white wine
2 tsp. dried oregano
1 tsp. dried basil
1/2 tsp. dried rosemary, crumbled
2 cloves garlic, minced
1/2 tsp. black pepper

Combine all ingredients in a glass or ceramic dish. Add poultry and marinate for 30 minutes at room temperature, or up to 8 hours in the refrigerator, turning occasionally. Discard remaining marinade.

MINT MARINADE FOR LAMB

If you like mint jelly with your lamb, try this marinade on some chops. You'll love the flavors.

½ cup finely chopped fresh mint leaves
¼ cup white wine
1 tbs. freshly squeezed lemon juice
½ cup vegetable oil
½ tsp. salt

Combine all ingredients in a glass or ceramic dish. Add lamb and marinate for 30 minutes at room temperature, or up to 8 hours in the refrigerator, turning occasionally. Discard remaining marinade.

MARINADE FOR PORK

This is a very simple, slightly sweet marinade for all cuts of pork. You can still serve savory side dishes with this—the small amount of brown sugar used only enhances the pork's natural tastes and doesn't overly sweeten the meat.

½ cup white wine
½ cup water
3 tbs. apple cider vinegar
1 tbs. brown sugar, packed
½ tsp. garlic salt

Combine all ingredients in a glass or ceramic dish. Add pork and marinate for 30 minutes at room temperature, or up to 8 hours in the refrigerator, turning occasionally. Discard remaining marinade.

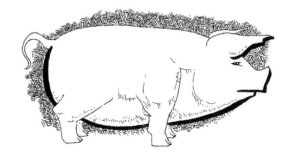

ORANGE GINGER MARINADE FOR PORK OR POULTRY

This is similar to teriyaki sauce, except it is much lighter and fresher tasting. Make a batch for marinating, and make a second batch to baste and glaze for even more flavor.

1 cup freshly squeezed orange juice
2 tbs. brown sugar, packed
2 tbs. grated fresh ginger
2 tbs. soy sauce

Combine all ingredients in a glass or ceramic dish. Add pork or poultry and marinate for 30 minutes at room temperature, or up to 8 hours in the refrigerator, turning occasionally. Discard remaining marinade.

RED WINE MARINADE FOR BEEF

This is a great marinade for large roasts (you'll need to double or triple the amounts if marinating a whole roast). Let your roast marinate overnight for maximum flavor.

1 cup red wine
¼ cup water or beef broth
2 cloves garlic, minced
2 tbs. Worcestershire sauce
½ tsp. freshly ground pepper

Combine all ingredients in a glass or ceramic dish. Add beef and marinate for 30 minutes at room temperature, or up to 8 hours in the refrigerator, turning occasionally. Discard remaining marinade.

TUSCAN BEEF MARINADE

My father was born and raised in the Tuscany region of Italy. This is an old family recipe that works on most cuts of steak.

½ cup finely chopped fresh basil leaves
¼ cup finely chopped fresh Italian parsley leaves
1 clove garlic, finely minced
¼ cup red wine vinegar
½ cup olive oil
½ tsp. salt
¼ tsp. freshly ground black pepper

Combine all ingredients in a glass or ceramic dish. Add beef and marinate for 30 minutes at room temperature, or up to 8 hours in the refrigerator, turning occasionally. Discard remaining marinade.

WHISKY MARINADE FOR RIBS

This is great on either pork or beef ribs. And it is much less messy than ribs cooked with a thick barbecue sauce.

1/3 cup whiskey
1/4 cup brown sugar, packed
1/4 cup apple juice
1/4 cup Dijon mustard

Combine all ingredients in a glass or ceramic dish. Add ribs and marinate for 1 hour at room temperature, or up to 8 hours in the refrigerator, turning occasionally. Baste ribs frequently with marinade while cooking. Discard remaining marinade.

STEAKS, CHOPS, KABOBS AND MORE

31   Cooking Small Cuts of Meat or Poultry
32   Better Than Buffalo Wings
33   Sesame Chicken Skewers With Dipping Sauce
34   Rosemary Chicken Breasts
35   Pineapple Chicken
36   Lemon Basil Chicken
37   Cumin Chicken Skewers
38   Glistening Kung Pao Chicken
39   Orange Teriyaki Chicken
40   Herbed Turkey Burgers
41   Spring Lamb Shish Kabobs
42   Tarragon Lamb Kabobs
43   Lamb Chops With Red Peppers

- **44** Lamb Burgers
- **45** Sausages and Veggies
- **46** Chinese BBQ Pork Ribs
- **47** Jamaican Pork Chops
- **48** Pork Chops With Bourbon and Peaches
- **49** Pork Chops With Citrus Salsa
- **50** Veal Chops With Sage
- **51** Western BBQ Burgers
- **52** Beef Saté Skewers
- **54** Steaks With Sherried Mushrooms
- **56** Korean Beef Skewers
- **57** Pepper-Crusted T-Bones

COOKING SMALL CUTS OF MEAT OR POULTRY

Many rotisserie ovens come with multiple cooking accessories, such as skewers, racks, baking sheets and baskets. These accessories give you the flexibility to cook smaller cuts of meats and poultry, and in less time than a large piece of meat. You still get the benefits of constant basting and even cooking. If you are using a rub or chunky marinade, your flavors will not be left sticking to the grill, but will cling to your meal. I have found that boneless, skinless chicken breasts are more tender and juicy when cooked in the rotisserie than by any other method.

Since the thickness of the meat will vary along with the temperature controls of your oven, testing your meats and poultry for doneness is critical here. Use instant-read thermometers when approaching the estimated time. And always discard remaining marinades and basting sauces. These should only be used while cooking the meats and poultry, and never on the meat after you have removed it from the oven.

BETTER THAN BUFFALO WINGS

Servings: 4–6

I love Buffalo wings, but hate cooking them. Deep-frying in oil or shortening and then coating them in butter makes them a calorie bomb! Try this recipe instead for great spicy wings.

1/2 cup Tabasco Sauce or other hot pepper sauce
2 tbs. cayenne pepper
1 tsp. salt
20 chicken wing "drummettes"

Mix together hot pepper sauce, cayenne pepper and salt. Place wings in the rotisserie basket and brush with hot pepper sauce mixture. Cook for about 15 minutes, until done and skin is crispy. Baste often with remaining sauce.

SESAME CHICKEN SKEWERS WITH DIPPING SAUCE

This is a version of "yakitori" with a simple sauce in which to dip the bite-sized pieces of chicken.

4 boneless, skinless chicken breast halves
2 tbs. vegetable oil
1 tbs. sesame oil
¼ cup sesame seeds
½ cup soy sauce
3 tbs. brown sugar, packed
3 tbs. rice wine vinegar
1 green onion, slivered

Cut chicken into medium chunks about 1- to 1½-inches square. In a medium bowl, combine oils and add chicken chunks. Toss to coat. Thread chicken on 8 skewers and sprinkle seeds over chicken chunks. Cook for about 30 to 40 minutes, until chicken reaches 175.° While chicken is cooking, prepare dipping sauce.

In a small bowl, combine soy sauce, brown sugar, rice wine vinegar and green onions. Stir to mix and set aside. Keep at room temperature for dipping.

ROSEMARY CHICKEN BREASTS

Servings: 4

This is also delicious using chicken quarters or leg-thigh pieces.

1/2 tsp. salt
2 tbs. fresh rosemary, minced
2 cloves garlic, minced
1/4 cup olive oil
2 tbs. white wine
4 chicken breast halves

Mix together all ingredients and marinate chicken for 15 minutes. Place breasts in the rotisserie basket. Cook for about 30 to 45 minutes, until chicken is done, basting with remaining marinade. Discard any remaining marinade.

PINEAPPLE CHICKEN

Servings: 4

Sweet glazed chicken with fresh pineapple spears make an attractive entrée.

1 cup pineapple juice
¼ cup brown sugar, packed
1 tsp. ground ginger
1 fresh pineapple, peeled, cored and cut into quarters
1 fryer chicken, cut into quarters

Mix together pineapple juice, brown sugar and ginger and stir until sugar is dissolved. Arrange pineapple pieces and chicken in the rotisserie basket. Baste with pineapple glaze and place in the rotisserie oven. Continue basting frequently, until chicken is cooked, about 30 to 45 minutes. Discard any remaining glaze.

LEMON BASIL CHICKEN

Servings: 4

This recipe can also be adapted for use with any firm-fleshed fish.

juice of 2 lemons
grated zest of 1 lemon
1/4 cup butter, melted
1 tsp. dried basil
1/2 tsp. garlic salt
1 chicken, cut into pieces

Mix together all ingredients and marinate chicken for 15 minutes. Place chicken in the rotisserie basket. Cook for about 30 to 45 minutes, until chicken is done, basting with remaining marinade. Discard any remaining marinade.

CUMIN CHICKEN SKEWERS

Servings: 4–6

You can use boneless, skinless chicken thighs or even turkey, if you prefer. Try serving on top of Spanish rice for a complete meal.

4 boneless, skinless chicken breast halvess
½ cup vegetable oil
2 tsp. garlic salt
1 tsp. chili powder
4 tsp. ground cumin
2 yellow onions

Cut chicken into medium chunks, about 1- to 1½-inch squares. In a medium bowl, combine oil, garlic salt, chili powder and cumin. Add chicken and toss to coat. Marinate for 15 minutes.

Peel and vertically quarter onions. Cut each wedge in half horizontally, to make large chunks. Thread chicken and onion chunks on skewers (depending on how large each breast is, you may need to use 2 or 3 pieces of chicken for each onion chunk). Drizzle remaining marinade over onion wedges to coat. Cook for about 30 to 40 minutes, until chicken reaches 175.°

GLISTENING KUNG PAO CHICKEN

Servings: 4–6

If you like the hot and spicy flavor of kung pao chicken, try this recipe for chicken pieces. If possible, marinate the chicken for 24 hours before cooking.

2 tsp. red pepper flakes
¼ cup vegetable oil
2 tbs. soy sauce
1 tbs. sesame oil
1 tbs. granulated sugar
1 fryer chicken, cut into pieces

Mix together all ingredients except chicken and stir until sugar is dissolved. Place chicken in a nonmetal dish and pour marinade over. Marinate chicken for at least 4 hours in the refrigerator, or up to 24 hours. Reserve marinade for basting.

Place chicken pieces in the rotisserie basket. Cook for about 30 to 45 minutes, basting frequently with marinade, until chicken is done. Discard any remaining marinade.

ORANGE TERIYAKI CHICKEN

Servings: 6–8

The use of orange juice in this teriyaki recipe gives it a new fresh flavor.

1 1/2 cups freshly squeezed orange juice
grated zest of 1 orange
1 1/2 cups brown sugar, packed
1 cup soy sauce
2 tsp. ground ginger
1 chicken, cut into pieces

Combine orange juice, zest, sugar, soy sauce and ginger in a large bowl. Add chicken and toss to mix evenly. Cover and refrigerate for 1 to 2 hours.

Remove chicken from marinade and place in the rotisserie basket. Cook for about 30 to 45 minutes, until chicken is done, basting often with remaining marinade. Discard any remaining marinade.

HERBED TURKEY BURGERS

Servings: 4

These burgers are mildly seasoned with fresh herbs. Try serving on Kaiser rolls, with a dollop of good-quality mayonnaise or Dijon mustard.

1 lb. ground turkey
2 tbs. minced fresh chives
1 tbs. minced fresh rosemary
2 tbs. minced fresh parsley
1 tsp. salt
½ tsp. freshly ground black pepper

Combine all ingredients and set aside for 15 minutes. Form into 4 patties. Place burgers in the rotisserie basket. Cook for about 15 to 20 minutes, checking for doneness. Internal temperature should be at 180° when burgers are done.

SPRING LAMB SHISH KABOBS

Servings: 8

This is a very traditional way of preparing lamb chunks on skewers—simple and delicious.

1 clove garlic, minced
½ cup olive oil
½ cup freshly squeezed lemon juice
¼ cup minced fresh rosemary
½ tsp. salt

2 lb. lamb, cut into 1-inch cubes
2 red onions
2 red bell peppers
16 cherry tomatoes

Combine garlic, olive oil, lemon juice, rosemary and salt in a medium bowl. Add lamb to mixture and marinate for 15 minutes.

Peel and cut onions into vertical quarters and cut each quarter in half for a total of 16 pieces. Cut bell peppers as you did onions.

Thread lamb, onions, peppers and tomatoes on 16 skewers. Cook until lamb is done, about 15 minutes for medium. Check for desired doneness.

TARRAGON LAMB KABOBS

Servings: 8

Traditional Greek flavors and bright vegetables make these kabobs perfect for spring and summer meals.

¼ cup chopped fresh tarragon
¼ cup olive oil
¼ cup red wine vinegar
1 clove garlic, minced
¼ tsp. salt
2 lb. lamb, cut into 1-inch cubes
16 cherry tomatoes

Combine tarragon, oil, vinegar, garlic and salt in a medium bowl. Add lamb to mixture and marinate for 15 minutes.

Thread lamb and tomatoes on 16 skewers. Cook until lamb is done, about 15 minutes for medium. Check for desired doneness.

LAMB CHOPS WITH RED PEPPERS

Servings: 4

Red bell peppers are very sweet when cooked and complement the tender lamb chops.

4 lamb chops, about 1 inch thick
1/4 cup olive oil
1/4 cup fresh thyme leaves
1/2 tsp. garlic salt
2 red bell peppers, quartered

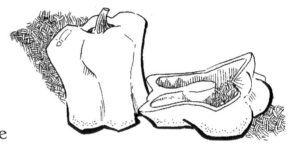

Rub chops with olive oil. Sprinkle thyme leaves and garlic salt on meat and press in lightly. Place chops and red bell peppers in the rotisserie basket. Cook until lamb is done, about 20 minutes for medium. Check for desired doneness.

LAMB BURGERS

Servings: 4

Ground lamb, with a little seasoning, makes more tender and juicy burgers than plain beef. For a different burger meal, serve on buns with cucumbers and yogurt.

1 lb. ground lamb
1/4 cup minced yellow onion
1 tsp. salt
1/2 tsp. freshly ground black pepper
3 tbs. red wine

Combine all ingredients and let stand for 15 minutes. Form into 4 patties. Place burgers in the rotisserie basket. Cook for about 10 to 15 minutes for medium, checking for doneness.

SAUSAGES AND VEGGIES

Servings: 4

If you have ever cooked sausages on a grill, you know how the fat drips off and causes flare-ups. Cooking them in the rotisserie is the perfect way to get great-tasting sausages.

4 large, uncooked sausages (such as Italian style, chorizo, or flavored)
1 large red onion
8 large white mushrooms

Place sausages in the rotisserie basket. Peel and quarter red onion and place in basket with sausages. Arrange mushrooms around sausages and onion quarters.
Cook for about 30 to 40 minutes, until sausages reach 175.°

CHINESE BBQ PORK RIBS

These ribs get their Chinese flavor from marinating in hoisin sauce and spices.

1 cup hoisin sauce
1/2 tsp. white pepper
1/2 cup white wine
1 clove garlic, minced
4 lb. country-style pork ribs

In a large locking plastic bag, mix together hoisin sauce, pepper, wine and garlic. Add ribs and marinate overnight, turning once. Reserve marinade for basting.

Place ribs in the rotisserie basket. Cook for about 1 to 1 1/2 hours, basting frequently with marinating liquid. Discard any remaining marinade.

JAMAICAN PORK CHOPS

Servings: 4

Jamaican "jerk" pork is hot, Hot, HOT and spicy. This has many of the flavors of jerk pork, but with minimum fire.

1 tsp. garlic salt
1 cup pineapple juice
1 1/2 tsp. ground ginger
1/4 tsp. cayenne pepper
1/2 tsp. ground allspice
1 tsp. cinnamon
1/2 tsp. ground nutmeg
1/2 cup brown sugar, packed
1/2 cup cider vinegar
3 tbs. soy sauce
4 thick-cut boneless pork chops
salt and pepper to taste

In a medium saucepan, combine all ingredients except pork chops. Set mixture over medium heat and bring to a boil. Set aside.

Season pork chops with salt and pepper on both sides. Place in the rotisserie basket and cook until internal temperature is 160,° basting with sauce frequently. Serve with any remaining sauce drizzled over the top.

PORK CHOPS WITH BOURBON AND PEACHES

Servings: 4

The bourbon in this recipe flavors both pork and peaches.

1/4 cup honey
1 tbs. soy sauce
1/4 cup bourbon
4 boneless pork chops, about 1/2 inch thick
4 fresh peaches, peeled and halved

In a shallow bowl, combine honey, soy sauce and bourbon. To make mixing easier, heat the marinade for a few seconds in your microwave, or pour into a small saucepan and heat on your stovetop. Add chops and marinate at room temperature for 30 minutes, turning once.

Place chops and peaches in the rotisserie basket. Cook, basting chops and peaches frequently with remaining marinade. Pork will be done in about 20 minutes.

PORK CHOPS WITH CITRUS SALSA

Servings: 4

Sweet yet spicy, this salsa goes well with most cuts of pork.

4 thin-cut, boneless pork chops
3 tbs. olive oil
grated zest of 1 lime
½ tsp. salt
2 large seedless oranges
¼ cup lime juice
¼ cup lemon juice
1 small red onion, minced
1 jalapeño pepper, seeded and minced
¼ cup minced fresh cilantro

Rub pork chops with olive oil. Press lime zest into meat and sprinkle with salt. Place chops in the rotisserie basket. Cook for about 10 minutes, checking for doneness.

While chops are cooking, prepare salsa. Peel oranges and break into segments. Cut each segment into small, bite-sized pieces. In a medium nonmetal bowl, mix oranges with lime juice, lemon juice, onion, jalapeño pepper and cilantro. Let stand at room temperature and serve with chops.

VEAL CHOPS WITH SAGE

Servings: 4

Use only fresh sage for this recipe, as you want a delicate flavor on the tender chops.

4 veal chops with bone, 10–12 oz. each
1/4 cup olive oil
1/4 cup minced fresh sage
1 tsp. garlic salt

Rub veal chops with olive oil. Press sage into meat and sprinkle with garlic salt. Place chops in the rotisserie basket. Cook for about 20 minutes for rare, or to desired doneness.

WESTERN BBQ BURGERS

Servings: 4

Who needs a smoky barbecue to get great-tasting, tender burgers? Use your favorite barbecue sauce.

1 lb. ground beef
½ cup barbecue sauce
¼ cup cooked, crumbled bacon
¼ cup breadcrumbs

Mix all ingredients together. Form 4 patties, being careful not to overwork beef. Place in the rotisserie basket and cook for about 20 minutes, until done; internal temperature should be 160.° Serve plain or on buns.

BEEF SATÉ SKEWERS

Servings: 8

There are hundreds of versions of satés, for beef, chicken and fish. This is a slightly sweet saté with lots of flavor. This can also be served as an appetizer for 16.

2 lb. beef chunks, about 1 inch square
½ cup chopped fresh cilantro
2 cloves garlic, minced
½ cup soy sauce
½ cup light brown sugar, packed

Combine beef chunks with cilantro, garlic, soy sauce and brown sugar in a medium bowl and stir to mix, until brown sugar has dissolved. Marinate for 30 minutes at room temperature, stirring once or twice. Reserve marinade for basting.

Thread beef onto skewers. Place in the rotisserie and cook to desired doneness, about 30 minutes for medium. Baste often with remaining marinade.

Arrange on a serving plate when done. Discard any remaining marinade.

STEAKS WITH SHERRIED MUSHROOMS

Servings: 4

Steak and mushrooms are a classic pair and this version is dressed-up enough to serve guests. Use a variety of fresh mushrooms, such as cremini, oyster and shiitake, along with white mushrooms for a more dramatic entrée.

4 rib-eye steaks, ¾ inch thick
8 tsp. olive oil
2 tsp. garlic salt
2 tsp. freshly ground pepper
3 tbs. butter
¼ cup minced yellow onion
1 lb. sliced mushrooms
½ cup sherry
½ cup whipping cream
¼ cup minced fresh chives

Rub each steak with 2 tsp. of the olive oil. Sprinkle each side of each steak with $1/4$ tsp. of the garlic salt and $1/4$ tsp. of the pepper. Place steaks in the rotisserie basket. Cook to desired doneness, about 20 minutes for medium.

While steaks cook, prepare mushrooms. In a medium skillet, melt butter over medium-high heat. Add onion and sauté until translucent, about 2 minutes. Add mushrooms and sauté until mushrooms' moisture has evaporated and they begin to brown, about 15 minutes. Add sherry and continue to cook until sherry has evaporated. Reduce heat to low and add cream, simmering until cream thickens, about 1 minute.

Arrange steaks on a serving platter. Cover steaks with mushrooms and sprinkle with chives. Serve immediately.

KOREAN BEEF SKEWERS

Servings: 4

You can also cut the beef into larger, 1-inch cubes if you prefer—just allow a bit more cooking time.

1/2 cup sherry
1/4 cup soy sauce
4 tsp. sesame oil
4 green onions, thinly sliced
1 lb. beef round steak or London broil

Combine sherry, soy sauce, sesame oil and green onions in a shallow dish. Slice beef into 1/4-inch-thick strips. Add beef to sherry mixture and marinate for 15 minutes.

Thread beef on skewers. Place skewers in the rotisserie and cook for about 15 minutes, until beef is done. Check for desired doneness.

PEPPER-CRUSTED T-BONES

Servings: 4

The peppercorn blend gives a nice bite to the steaks. Peppercorn blend usually contains white, black, green and pink peppercorns.

4 T-bone steaks, about 1 1/2 inches thick
8 tsp. olive oil
2 tsp. garlic salt
4 tsp. freshly ground peppercorn blend

Rub each steak with 2 tsp. of the olive oil. Sprinkle each side of each steak with 1/4 tsp. of the garlic salt and 1/2 tsp. of the pepper. Place steaks in the rotisserie basket. Cook until desired doneness, about 25 minutes for medium.

LARGE CUTS OF MEAT

59 Large Cuts of Meat on the Rotisserie
60 Herbed Sirloin Roast
61 Jack Daniel's Roast
62 Rib Eye Roast With Madeira
63 Prime Rib With Horseradish Sauce
64 Mustard Pork Roast
65 Maple-Glazed Pork Loin
66 Cuban Pork Loin
67 Pork Loin With Cranberries
68 Pork Roast With Sage
69 Pork With Herbs
70 Rosemary Leg of Lamb

LARGE CUTS OF MEAT ON THE ROTISSERIE

Large cuts of meat require a bit more time in the rotisserie than in traditional ovens, but the result is a far juicier and more flavorful meal.

When cooking heavier cuts of meat, it is critical to get your food evenly balanced on the rotisserie bar. You will get uneven cooking if the bar is not placed in the center of your food. Unbalanced loads also create much more work for the rotisserie motor.

HERBED SIRLOIN ROAST

Servings: 6–8

This roast is so flavorful and juicy that you won't miss having a gravy or sauce to pass with the meat.

½ cup olive oil
½ cup red wine
1 tsp. dried thyme
1 tsp. dried sage

2 cloves garlic, minced
½ tsp. black pepper
3–4 lb. sirloin tip roast, trimmed of excess fat

In a large locking plastic bag, or in a bowl large enough to hold the roast, combine all ingredients except meat. Mix well and add roast. Marinate for a minimum of 8 hours or overnight in the refrigerator. Remove from refrigerator 30 minutes before cooking.

Place meat on the rotisserie bar and secure with tines. Roast until internal temperature is 145° for rare, 160° for medium or 170° for well done. This will take about 45 to 90 minutes, depending on size. Let stand for 10 minutes before removing rotisserie bar and carving.

JACK DANIEL'S ROAST

Servings: 6–8

I love this sweet and tender roast. Marinating for 24 hours is critical.

½ cup Jack Daniel's whiskey
½ cup brown sugar, packed
¼ cup soy sauce
1 tbs. Liquid Smoke
2 cloves garlic, minced
1 boneless beef roast, 2–3 lb.

In a large locking plastic bag, combine whiskey, brown sugar, soy sauce, Liquid Smoke and garlic. Add roast and squeeze out air. Place in the refrigerator and marinate for 24 hours, turning once.

Place roast on the rotisserie bar and secure with tines. Roast for about 1 hour for medium (check temperature for doneness—medium is 160°), basting occasionally with remaining marinade. Remove from oven and let stand for 10 minutes before carving. Discard remaining marinade.

RIB EYE ROAST WITH MADEIRA

Servings: 10–12

You don't need pan drippings to make a flavorful sauce or gravy, as long as you use a good quality broth as your base. And always use good quality wine when cooking; if it isn't good enough to drink, it's not good enough to cook with.

1 boneless beef rib eye roast, 4–6 lb.
1 tsp. garlic salt
1 tsp. onion powder
1 tsp. freshly ground black pepper
1 cup beef broth
¼ cup Madeira wine
1 tbs. catsup

Place beef on the rotisserie bar and secure with tines. Sprinkle garlic salt, onion powder and pepper on meat and rub in lightly. Roast for about 1 hour for medium (check temperature for doneness—medium is 160°). Remove from oven and let stand for 10 minutes while you prepare sauce.

In a small saucepan, combine beef broth, wine and catsup. Bring to a boil over medium high heat and cook until reduced to ¾ cup. Serve with beef.

PRIME RIB WITH HORSERADISH SAUCE

Servings: 6–8

Instead of serving the beef with pan juices ("au jus"), serve with a creamy, mildly flavored horseradish sauce.

1 cup sour cream
¼ cup commercially prepared horseradish sauce
1 tbs. minced fresh chives
1 prime rib roast, 3–4 lb.
2 tsp. garlic salt
1 tsp. pepper

Prepare horseradish sauce by combining sour cream, horseradish and chives in a small bowl. Stir to mix well, cover and refrigerate while beef is prepared.

Remove roast from refrigerator at least 30 minutes before cooking. Season beef with garlic salt and pepper. Place meat on the rotisserie bar and secure with tines. Roast until internal temperature is 145° for rare, 160° for medium or 170° for well done: about 60 to 90 minutes, depending on size. Let stand for 10 minutes before removing rotisserie bar and carving.

MUSTARD PORK ROAST

Servings: 6–8

You can use any type of spicy mustard in this recipe. My favorite is a grained mustard, flavored with a bit of horseradish.

3 tbs. spicy mustard
1 tbs. olive oil
1 boneless pork roast, 3–4 lb.

Mix mustard and oil together and spread on all sides of roast.

Place meat on the rotisserie bar and secure with tines. Roast until internal temperature is 150°, about 90 minutes to 2 hours, depending on size. Let stand for 10 minutes before removing rotisserie bar and carving.

MAPLE-GLAZED PORK LOIN

Servings: 6–8

This is a perfect autumn entrée. Be sure to use only pure maple syrup and not "pancake" syrup, which is really just corn syrup with maple flavoring.

½ cup apple juice
¼ cup maple syrup
¼ cup brown sugar, packed
½ yellow onion, minced
1 bay leaf

1 pork loin, about 1½–2 lb.
2 tbs. butter
½ cup maple syrup
¼ cup apple juice

In a large locking plastic bag, mix together apple juice, maple syrup, brown sugar, onion and bay leaf. Add pork loin and marinate for 8 hours or overnight.

When ready to cook meat, prepare glaze. Combine butter, maple syrup and apple juice in a small saucepan. Heat mixture over low heat until butter has melted and mixture is smooth. Let cool before using.

Place meat on the rotisserie bar and secure with tines. Discard marinade. Roast until internal temperature is 150°, about 30 minutes depending on size. Baste frequently with prepared glaze.

Let stand for 10 minutes before removing rotisserie bar and carving.

CUBAN PORK LOIN

Servings: 6–8

This pork loin is spicy, a bit sweet and a bit hot—great with margaritas!

1 tbs. ground cumin
1 tbs. chili powder
1 tbs. garlic salt
1 tsp. cinnamon
1 tbs. brown sugar
1 tsp. cayenne pepper
1 pork tenderloin, about 1½–2 lb.

In a small bowl, combine cumin, chili powder, garlic salt, cinnamon, brown sugar and cayenne pepper. Rub spice mixture on all sides of pork.

Place meat on the rotisserie bar and secure with tines. Roast until internal temperature is 150°; about 30 minutes, depending on size. Let stand for 10 minutes before removing rotisserie bar and carving.

PORK LOIN WITH CRANBERRIES

Servings: 6–8

Many people serve cranberry sauce with simple pork dishes, but try this recipe with fresh cranberries—you'll never want to use canned again!

4 cups fresh or frozen cranberries
1 cup apple juice
1 1/2 cups granulated sugar
2 tsp. minced fresh ginger
1 pork tenderloin, 1–2 lb.
1 tbs. vegetable oil
1 tsp. ground ginger

In a medium saucepan, combine cranberries, apple juice, sugar and ginger. Cook over medium heat until mixture boils and cranberries have burst, about 20 minutes. Transfer to a bowl, cover and chill. Sauce will gel upon cooling.

Rub pork with oil and sprinkle with ground ginger. Place meat on the rotisserie bar and secure with tines. Roast until internal temperature is 150°, about 30 minutes depending on size. Let stand for 10 minutes before removing rotisserie bar and carving. Serve cranberry sauce at room temperature or heated.

PORK ROAST WITH SAGE

Servings: 6–8

Pork roasts cooked in the rotisserie come out much juicier than oven-roasted meats. The fresh sage is inserted into small cuts in the meat.

1 boneless pork roast, 3–4 lb.
10 fresh sage leaves
1 tbs. olive oil
2 tsp. garlic salt

Using a sharp pointed knife, make 10 evenly spaced 2-inch slits in pork. With the tip of the knife, insert 1 sage leaf into each slit. Rub pork with olive oil and sprinkle with garlic salt.

Place meat on the rotisserie bar and secure with tines. Roast until internal temperature is 150,° about 90 minutes to 2 hours, depending on size. Let stand for 10 minutes before removing rotisserie bar and carving.

PORK WITH HERBS

Servings: 6–8

The secret to this recipe is the overnight marinating of the pork roast.

½ cup white wine
½ cup minced fresh Italian parsley
¼ cup minced fresh chives
2 tbs. chopped fresh basil
2 cloves garlic, minced
1 boneless pork roast, 3–4 lb.

    In a medium bowl, combine wine, parsley, chives, basil and garlic. Add roast and turn to coat. Cover tightly and refrigerate overnight or for a minimum of 8 hours, turning once.
    Place meat on the rotisserie bar and secure with tines. Discard marinade. Roast until internal temperature is 160,° about 75 minutes to 2 hours, depending on size. Let stand for 10 minutes before removing rotisserie bar and carving.

ROSEMARY LEG OF LAMB

Servings: 8–10

Lamb is frequently paired with rosemary or mint. I always like to use fresh rosemary, because the taste is milder than dried rosemary.

1 butterflied leg of lamb, about 5 lb.
10 small sprigs fresh rosemary
2 tsp. freshly ground black pepper
2 tsp. garlic salt
1 tbs. minced fresh rosemary

Cut 10 evenly spaced slits into the lamb and insert a rosemary sprig into each cut. Mix together pepper, garlic salt and minced rosemary and rub into both sides of lamb. Using butcher twine, securely tie lamb into a long, cylindrical shape.

Place lamb on the rotisserie bar and secure with tines. Roast until internal temperature is 160,° about 1½ to 2 hours. Let stand for 10 minutes before removing rotisserie bar and carving lamb.

WHOLE POULTRY

- **72** The Rotisserie and Whole Poultry
- **73** Apricot-Glazed Chicken
- **74** Country Herbed Chicken
- **75** Lemon Lime Chicken
- **76** Hot Honey Chicken
- **78** Moroccan Stuffed Chicken
- **80** Smoky Bacon Chicken
- **81** Super Spicy Chicken
- **82** Fresh Herb Rotisserie Turkey
- **84** Curry Game Hens With Kiwi Salsa
- **86** Mustard Maple Turkey Breasts
- **87** Ginger and Honey Game Hens
- **88** Orange Bourbon Hens

THE ROTISSERIE AND WHOLE POULTRY

Whole poultry requires a bit more time in the rotisserie than in traditional ovens, but the result is a far juicier and more flavorful meal. When cooking large birds, it is critical to get your food evenly balanced on the rotisserie bar. You will get uneven cooking if the bar is not placed in the center of your bird. Unbalanced loads also create much more work for the rotisserie motor.

APRICOT-GLAZED CHICKEN

Servings: 6–8

Apricots are used to flavor this chicken, both inside and out.

1 cup dried apricots
1 cup boiling water
1 roasting chicken, 4–5 lb.

1 cup apricot preserves
2 tbs. honey
½ cup white wine

Place dried apricots in a medium bowl and add boiling water. Cover with a lid or plastic wrap and set aside for 30 minutes. Place rehydrated apricots inside chicken's cavity. Secure cavity with tines or with string. Discard remaining water.

In a small saucepan, combine preserves, honey and white wine. Heat over medium heat until smooth, stirring frequently. Keep warm.

Place chicken on the rotisserie bar and secure with tines. Tie legs and wings with cooking string to prevent them from touching heating elements. Cook for about 30 minutes before first basting of glaze. Continue basting every 30 minutes until chicken is done, or you have used all glaze. Roast until internal temperature is 180°, about 1½ to 2 hours. Let stand for 10 minutes before removing rotisserie bar and carving. Remove apricots from cavity and discard before serving.

COUNTRY HERBED CHICKEN

Servings: 6–8

The simple herb mix in this recipe accents the chicken without overpowering it. You'll have a beautiful chicken to carve, and one that is incredibly moist and tender.

½ tsp. poultry seasoning
¼ tsp. dried thyme
¼ tsp. dried sage
¼ tsp. garlic salt

2 cloves garlic, cut in half
2 bay leaves
1 roasting chicken, 4–5 lb.

In a small bowl, combine poultry seasoning, thyme, sage and garlic salt. Rub herb blend onto chicken's skin (if desired, you can also put herbs under skin). Place garlic cloves and bay leaves inside chicken's cavity.

Place chicken on the rotisserie bar and secure with tines. Tie legs and wings with cooking string to prevent them from touching heating elements. Roast until internal temperature is 180°, about 1½ to 2 hours. Let stand for 10 minutes before removing rotisserie bar and carving.

LEMON LIME CHICKEN

Servings: 6–8

Try serving this chicken with rice pilaf and butter-steamed sugar snap peas.

1 tbs. grated lime zest
1 tbs. grated lemon zest
1/4 cup freshly squeezed lime juice
1/4 cup freshly squeezed lemon juice
1 clove garlic, minced
1 tsp. salt
1 roasting chicken, about 3–4 lb.

In a small bowl, combine grated zests, lime juice, lemon juice, garlic and salt. Set aside.

Place chicken on the rotisserie bar and secure with tines. Tie legs and wings with cooking string to prevent them from touching heating elements. Baste outside skin and inside cavity with lemon-lime mixture. Roast until internal temperature is 180°, about 1 1/2 to 2 hours, basting every 20 minutes until chicken is done. Let stand for 10 minutes before removing rotisserie bar and carving.

HOT HONEY CHICKEN

Servings: 6–8

This dish is sweet yet fiery! Take care when preparing jalapeño peppers—keep your hands away from your eyes.

2 jalapeño peppers, halved and seeded
1 roasting chicken, 4–5 lb.
½ cup honey
2 tbs. white wine
½ tsp. ground ginger
½ tsp. cayenne pepper

Place jalapeño peppers inside chicken's cavity. Secure cavity with tines or string.

In a small saucepan, combine honey, white wine, ginger and cayenne pepper. Heat over medium heat until smooth, stirring frequently. Keep warm.

Place chicken on the rotisserie bar and secure with tines. Tie legs and wings with cooking string to prevent them from touching heating elements. Brush with honey glaze. Roast, continuing to baste every 20 minutes, until chicken is done, or you have used all glaze. Roast until internal temperature is 180,° about 1½ to 2 hours. Let stand for 10 minutes before removing rotisserie bar and carving. Remove peppers from cavity and discard before serving.

In a medium saucepan, mix chicken broth mixture with sherry. Bring mixture to a boil. Reduce heat and simmer for 20 minutes to reduce in volume. Combine ¼ cup chicken broth and flour in a small bowl and stir until smooth. Add to gravy mixture in saucepan. Bring mixture to a boil, stirring frequently. Add herbs and stir to mix. Serve immediately.

MOROCCAN STUFFED CHICKEN

Servings: 6–8

The sweet couscous stuffing in this recipe is the perfect accompaniment to cinnamon-scented chicken. Couscous is usually found near the pasta and rice in your grocery store.

2 cups chicken broth
1 cup couscous
½ cup raisins
¼ cup slivered almonds
1 tsp. ground cardamom
2 tsp. cinnamon
½ tsp. salt
1 roasting chicken, 5 lb.

In a medium saucepan, bring chicken broth to a boil. Add couscous, stir and remove from heat. Cover and let stand for 5 minutes. Stir in raisins and almonds. Set aside.

In a small bowl, combine cardamom, cinnamon and salt. Rub spice blend on chicken's skin (if desired, you can also put spices under skin). Place prepared couscous in chicken cavity and tie legs together.

Place chicken on the rotisserie bar and secure with tines. Tie wings with cooking string to prevent them from touching heating elements. Roast until internal temperature is 180,° about 1½ to 2 hours. Let stand for 10 minutes before removing rotisserie bar and carving.

SMOKY BACON CHICKEN

Servings: 6–8

Bacon is used here to flavor the chicken with a delicious smoky taste.

8 strips bacon
1 roasting chicken, 4–5 lb.
1 yellow onion, quartered
salt to taste

Cook bacon until just beginning to crisp. Drain and reserve bacon fat. Loosen skin of chicken and place a strip of bacon under skin of each breast. Place remaining 6 bacon strips and quartered onion in cavity and tie legs together. Rub chicken with reserved bacon fat and sprinkle lightly with salt.

Place chicken on the rotisserie bar and secure with tines. Tie wings with cooking string to prevent them from touching heating elements. Roast until internal temperature is 180,° about 1½ to 2 hours. Let stand for 10 minutes before removing rotisserie bar and carving. Remove and discard bacon and onion.

SUPER SPICY CHICKEN

Servings: 4–6

Be warned—this is a very spicy dish that will leave your lips tingling! If you don't like hot and spicy, you can tone this down by reducing the amount of cayenne pepper, or omitting it altogether if you prefer.

6 tbs. paprika
3 tbs. ground cayenne pepper
2 tbs. garlic salt
2 tsp. freshly ground black pepper
1 roasting chicken, 3–4 lb.

In a small bowl, combine paprika, cayenne pepper, garlic salt and black pepper. Stir to mix well. Sprinkle seasoning over entire chicken, including cavity. Use all of the seasoning mixture. You can also place some of the seasoning under chicken's skin, if you like.

Place chicken on the rotisserie bar, securing with tines. Tie wings with cooking string to prevent them from touching heating elements. Roast until done and internal temperature is 180,° about 90 minutes. Let stand for 10 minutes before carving.

FRESH HERB ROTISSERIE TURKEY

Servings: 10–12

The availability of whole turkeys year-round makes this an entrée you can prepare anytime. The fresh herb gravy needs no pan drippings for extra flavor.

2 tsp. minced chives
2 tbs. finely chopped fresh sage
1 tsp. chopped fresh lemon thyme
1 tsp. chopped fresh savory
1 turkey, 12 lb.

GRAVY
3¼ cups chicken broth, divided
⅓ cup sherry
4 tsp. flour
2 tbs. minced fresh parsley
1 tsp. minced fresh chives
1 tsp. chopped fresh lemon thyme

In a small bowl, combine chives, sage, lemon thyme and savory. Set aside 1 tsp. of the herb mixture for the turkey's cavity. Loosen skin of turkey. Gently place herb mixture between skin and meat. Sprinkle reserved herbs inside turkey's cavity.

Place turkey on the rotisserie bar and secure with tines. Tie wings with cooking string to prevent them from touching heating elements. Roast until internal temperature is 170,° about 3 to 4 hours. Let stand for 15 minutes before removing rotisserie bar and carving.

In a medium saucepan, combine 3 cups of the chicken broth mixture and sherry. Bring mixture to a boil. Reduce heat, and simmer for 20 minutes to reduce. Combine remaining 1/4 cup chicken broth and flour in a small bowl, and stir until smooth. Add to gravy mixture in saucepan. Bring mixture to a boil, stirring frequently. Add herbs and stir to mix. Serve immediately.

CURRY GAME HENS WITH KIWI SALSA

Servings: 2–4

It seems a strange combination: an Indian-flavored game hen with a Mexican salsa. It works, though. The sweet kiwi salsa can be thought of as a mild chutney to accompany the hens. If you can't find all the seasonings for the curry mix, you can use commercial curry powder. You will need about 3 tablespoons. But making your own curry mixture is easy, and far better tasting.

1 tbs. ground cumin
1 tbs. ground coriander
1 tsp. ground ginger
4 tsp. ground turmeric
½ tsp. cinnamon
2 Cornish game hens
8 kiwi fruit
¼ cup honey
¼ cup minced red onion
¼ tsp. red pepper flakes

Combine cumin, coriander, ginger, turmeric and cinnamon in a small bowl. Rub all surfaces of game hens with this mixture. Sprinkle any remaining curry mixture into game hen cavities. Place game hens on the rotisserie bar and firmly secure with tines. Cook for about 30 to 45 minutes, until done; internal temperature should be 170.° While hens are cooking, prepare salsa.

Peel kiwi fruit. Gently cut into ½-inch cubes and place in a small, nonmetallic bowl. Add honey, red onion and red pepper flakes and gently toss to mix. Let stand at room temperature until hens are done.

MUSTARD MAPLE TURKEY BREASTS

Servings: 4–6

A turkey breast of this size can serve 4 to 6 people; it's the perfect size when you want to serve turkey, but not the whole bird.

1 turkey breast, 4–6 lb.
2 tbs. olive oil
½ cup Dijon mustard
½ cup pure maple syrup
2 tbs. butter, melted

Rub turkey breast with olive oil. Pierce breast with the rotisserie bar and secure with tines (or use the rotisserie basket.)

Prepare basting sauce: In a small bowl, combine mustard, maple syrup and melted butter. If butter firms up while cooking turkey, warm slightly to melt and smooth out basting sauce.

Roast turkey breast for about 30 minutes before the first basting. Continue basting every 15 minutes until turkey is done. Roast until internal temperature is 180,° about 1 to 1½ hours. Discard any remaining basting sauce. Let stand for 10 minutes before removing rotisserie bar and carving.

GINGER AND HONEY GAME HENS

Servings: 4

The combination of fresh ginger and honey gives an Asian taste to these little birds.

¼ cup soy sauce
¼ cup honey
¼ cup sherry
3 tbs. minced fresh ginger
2 cloves garlic, minced
2 Cornish game hens

In a large bowl, mix together soy sauce, honey, sherry, ginger and garlic. Place game hens in marinade and marinate for a minimum of 2 hours. Depending on the size of your bowl, you may need to turn hens halfway through the marinating time.

Remove hens from marinade and pat dry. Discard marinade. Place hens on the rotisserie bar and secure with tines. Tie wings with cooking string to prevent them from touching heating elements. Roast until internal temperature is 170,° about 30 to 45 minutes. Let stand for 10 minutes before removing rotisserie bar. Cut each hen in half down the breastbone and back, to create a total of 4 halves.

ORANGE BOURBON HENS

Servings: 4

The orange juice and bourbon marinade really penetrates the meat of these tasty game hens. The skin will be a deep brown once cooked.

1 cup freshly squeezed orange juice
1 cup water
3 tbs. molasses
¼ cup bourbon
2 Cornish game hens

GRAVY
1½ cups chicken broth
2 tbs. brown sugar, packed
2 tbs. bourbon
2 tbs. chicken broth
4 tsp. flour
¼ tsp. grated orange zest

In a large bowl, mix together orange juice, water, molasses and bourbon. Place game hens in marinade. Marinate for a minimum of 2 hours. Depending on the size of your bowl, you may need to turn hens halfway through marinating time.

Remove hens from marinade and pat dry. Discard marinade. Place hens on the rotisserie bar and secure with tines. Tie wings with cooking string to prevent them from touching heating elements. Roast until internal temperature is 170,° about 30 to 45 minutes. Let stand for 10 minutes before removing rotisserie bar. Cut each hen in half down the breastbone and back, to create a total of 4 halves.

Prepare gravy: In a medium saucepan, combine chicken broth, brown sugar and bourbon. Bring mixture to a boil. Reduce heat and simmer for 15 minutes to reduce. Combine 2 tbs. chicken broth and flour in a small bowl and stir until smooth. Add to gravy mixture in saucepan. Bring mixture to a boil, stirring frequently. Add orange zest and stir to mix. Serve immediately.

SEAFOOD

92	The Ideal Method for Cooking Seafood
93	Cajun Snapper
94	Chili-Seasoned Salmon
95	Dijon Tuna Steaks
96	Garlic Scampi
97	Halibut With Spicy Salsa
98	Mixed Seafood Skewers
99	Pacific Rim Trout
100	Trout With Green Onions
101	Prosciutto Prawn Skewers
102	Provence Halibut
103	Red Snapper With Chives
104	Salmon With Avocado Salsa

- *105*   Salmon With Dill
- *106*   Salsa Verde Shark
- *107*   Scallop Kabobs
- *108*   Scallops With Herbed Butter
- *109*   Shark With Greek Olive Butter
- *110*   Soft-Shell Crabs With Lemon Cream Sauce
- *111*   Spicy Catfish
- *112*   Swordfish With Rosemary Butter
- *113*   Tarragon Tuna
- *114*   Tuna With Sake
- *115*   Tequila Shrimp
- *116*   Teriyaki Salmon
- *117*   Tuna With Lemon Butter

THE IDEAL METHOD FOR COOKING SEAFOOD

If you have ever tried to barbecue or grill fish, you know that it can be difficult. Even on an oiled grate, fish can stick. It is also hard to turn fish over without it breaking apart.

Cooking seafood with a rotisserie is ideal, as you don't have to worry about turning the fish; it will always cook evenly. If you spray your rotisserie basket with a non-stick spray prior to placing the fish, you will almost be guaranteed easy removal.

The best ways to cook seafood in a rotisserie are with skewers or in the basket. Even large chunks or whole fish should not be cooked on a rotisserie bar, as the fish will break apart as it nears the end of cooking.

CAJUN SNAPPER

Servings: 4

This has the flavors of "blackened" Cajun fish, but without the hassle of true blackening. This is spicy and hot, so serve with cold beer to help put out the fire.

1 tsp. garlic salt
1 tsp. onion powder
1 tsp. paprika
1 tsp. white pepper
1 tsp. cayenne pepper
1 tsp. Old Bay seasoning
1 lb. red snapper fillets

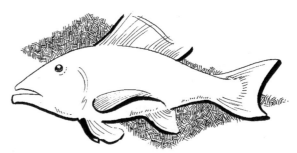

In a small bowl, combine garlic salt, onion powder, paprika, white pepper and Old Bay seasoning. Sprinkle over fish fillets and press in lightly. Let fish set for 30 minutes. Place in the rotisserie basket and cook for about 20 minutes, until opaque in the center.

CHILI-SEASONED SALMON

Servings: 4

After you make this recipe you'll have some of the spice mixture left over. It keeps well if stored in an airtight container.

1/4 cup paprika
1 tbs. chili powder
1 tbs. ground cumin
2 tsp. garlic salt
1/2 tsp. cayenne pepper
4 salmon fillets, about 6 oz. each
1/4 cup olive oil
1 cup commercially prepared tomato-based salsa

In a small bowl, combine paprika, chili powder, cumin, garlic salt and cayenne pepper. Rub fillets with olive oil and sprinkle with spice mixture, pressing in lightly. Let fish stand for 30 minutes. Place in the rotisserie basket and cook for about 20 minutes, until opaque in the center.

To serve, arrange fish on a serving platter and top with salsa.

DIJON TUNA STEAKS

Servings: 4

This way of cooking tuna steaks also works well with swordfish or shark steaks.

¼ cup freshly squeezed lemon juice
2 tbs. Dijon mustard
¼ tsp. salt
4 tuna steaks, about ½ inch thick

In a small bowl, combine lemon juice, mustard and salt. Pat mustard mixture onto both sides of tuna steaks. Arrange in the rotisserie basket. Cook for about 20 minutes, until opaque in the center.

GARLIC SCAMPI

Servings: 6

You can also serve this as an appetizer for 12.

1/4 cup butter, melted
1/4 cup olive oil
2 tbs. white wine
3 cloves garlic, pressed
2 lb. large shrimp, peeled and deveined
2 tbs. minced fresh chives

In a small bowl, combine butter, oil, wine and garlic. Thread shrimp onto skewers and brush with butter mixture. Cook for about 15 to 20 minutes, depending on size, until shrimp are pink. Baste frequently with butter mixture.

When done, remove from oven and sprinkle chives over shrimp. Discard any remaining butter mixture.

HALIBUT WITH SPICY SALSA

Servings: 4

Adding a few ingredients to your favorite commercial salsa creates a simple and flavorful sauce for this fish.

1 lb. halibut fillets
½ cup freshly squeezed lime juice
½ tsp. garlic salt
3 cups commercially prepared salsa
½ cup white wine
½ cup minced red onion
¼ cup minced fresh cilantro

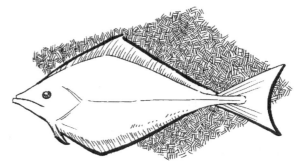

Rub halibut with lime juice and sprinkle with garlic salt. Arrange in the rotisserie basket and cook for about 20 minutes, until opaque in the center.

While fish is cooking, prepare salsa sauce: In a medium saucepan, combine salsa and wine. Bring to a boil over medium heat. Reduce heat to low and simmer for 10 minutes. Remove from heat and stir in onion and cilantro.

To serve, place fish on a serving platter and top with salsa.

MIXED SEAFOOD SKEWERS

Servings: 4–6

This is fun to serve, because you can easily let everyone try tastes of different fish. Choose as many types as you want from the list—or as few—making sure to have a total of 2 pounds of fish.

2 lb. boneless fish fillets (such as shark, mahi mahi, swordfish, monkfish, bass, or tuna)
1/4 cup olive oil
1/4 cup fresh lemon juice
1/4 cup minced fresh basil
1 clove garlic, minced

Cut fish into 1 1/2-inch cubes. In a medium bowl, combine oil, lemon juice, basil and garlic. Add fish and toss to coat.

Thread fish onto skewers and place in the rotisserie. Cook for about 20 minutes, or until fish is opaque in the center.

PACIFIC RIM TROUT

Servings: 4

Asian and Californian flavors blend together in this very flavorful trout dish.

4 trout fillets, about 6 oz. each
¼ cup vegetable oil
½ tsp. salt
½ cup butter
1 tbs. grated fresh ginger
1 tsp. grated lime zest
1 tsp. cayenne pepper
2 tbs. freshly squeezed lime juice

    Rub fish with vegetable oil and place in the rotisserie basket. Sprinkle with salt. Place basket in oven and cook for about 10 minutes, depending on size, until fish is opaque. While trout cooks, prepare drizzling sauce.
    In a small saucepan, melt butter over low heat. Add ginger and sauté until ginger becomes fragrant, but do not let brown. Remove from heat and stir in lime zest, cayenne pepper and lime juice.
    To serve, place trout on a serving platter and drizzle sauce over fish.

TROUT WITH GREEN ONIONS

Servings: 4

Fresh whole boned trout are usually available year-round. They have been cleaned and boned and therefore have a slit on one side that makes them easy to stuff. Here, simple green onions and a white wine butter flavor the fish. The bright green onions also look beautiful against the white fish.

4 green onions
4 whole boned trout, about 10 oz. each
2 tbs. butter
2 tbs. white wine
1/2 tsp. salt

Slice green onions into 2-inch pieces. Place one cut green onion in each trout.

Melt butter in a small saucepan over low heat. Remove from heat and add wine and salt. Let cool and then pour 1 tbs. of the mixture over onions.

Arrange fish in the basket and place in the rotisserie. Cook for about 10 minutes, until tender.

PROSCIUTTO PRAWN SKEWERS

Servings: 6

These simple skewers have a wonderful balance of flavors.

2 lb. large prawns, peeled and deveined
1/4 lb. prosciutto, cut into paper-thin slices
1 lb. cherry tomatoes
1 lb. white mushrooms, ends trimmed
1/4 cup butter, melted

Cut prosciutto into 6-x-2-inch strips. Wrap a slice of prosciutto around each prawn and thread prawns, cherry tomatoes and mushrooms onto skewers. Brush skewers with melted butter and place in the rotisserie. Cook for about 15 to 20 minutes, depending on size, until prawns are pink.

PROVENCE HALIBUT

Servings: 4

"Herbes de Provence" are used to create a paste rub on halibut steaks.

¼ cup fresh parsley
2 tbs. fresh sage
2 tbs. fresh rosemary
¼ cup fresh basil
2 tbs. fresh thyme
2 tbs. fresh savory
2 cloves garlic
¼ cup olive oil
2 tsp. salt
2 tsp. freshly ground black pepper
1 lb. halibut fillets

Place all ingredients, except halibut steaks, in a food processor or blender. Pulse until finely chopped, but not mushy. Lightly press herb mixture into fish. Place fish in the rotisserie basket and cook for about 20 minutes, until opaque in the center.

RED SNAPPER WITH CHIVES

Servings: 4

Lemon and chives flavor the snapper fillets and make a pretty presentation.

juice of 1 lemon
2 tbs. olive oil
4 red snapper fillets
½ cup minced fresh chives
½ tsp. salt

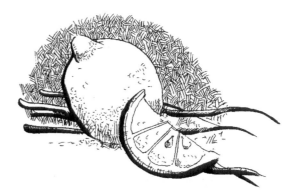

Mix together lemon juice and olive oil and rub over snapper fillets. Sprinkle chives over fish and finish with a sprinkle of salt. Place fillets in the rotisserie basket and cook for about 10 to 15 minutes, until done.

SALMON WITH AVOCADO SALSA

Servings: 4

No, this isn't another term for guacamole. The avocado is paired with lots of tomatoes and cilantro for a chunky salsa to top the lightly seasoned salmon.

1/4 cup olive oil
4 salmon fillets, about 8 oz. each
3/4 tsp. garlic salt
2 ripe avocados
2 ripe tomatoes, chopped (about 1 cup)

1/4 cup chopped red onion
2 tbs. freshly squeezed lemon juice
1/4 cup finely chopped fresh cilantro
1/2 tsp. ground cumin

Rub olive oil on salmon. Sprinkle with garlic salt and place in the rotisserie basket. Cook for about 20 minutes, until opaque in the center. While salmon is cooking, prepare salsa.

Peel and pit avocados and cut into small chunks. Mix gently together with tomatoes, red onion, lemon juice, cilantro and cumin, being careful that avocado chunks do not break apart. Keep at room temperature until ready to serve.

To serve, arrange salmon on a serving platter and top each fillet with a large scoop of salsa. Pass remaining salsa with fish.

SALMON WITH DILL

Servings: 4

Here's a great summer entrée—simple, fast and perfect with a glass of cold white wine.

1/4 cup olive oil
4 salmon fillets, about 8 oz. each
2 tbs. minced fresh dill
1 tbs. minced fresh chives
1/2 tsp. salt

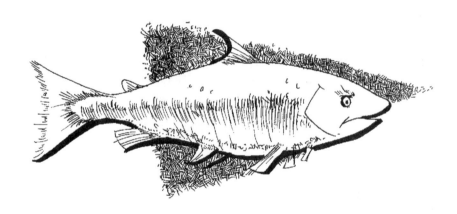

Rub olive oil on salmon and sprinkle with dill and chives. Pat herbs into surface lightly. Sprinkle with salt. Place in the rotisserie basket and cook for about 20 minutes, until opaque in the center.

SALSA VERDE SHARK

Servings: 4

Salsa verde is not a Mexican salsa, but Italian. This is a strongly flavored sauce and should be used on heartier fish steaks like shark, tuna and swordfish.

1 cup fresh Italian parsley leaves
3 tbs. capers, rinsed and drained
3 anchovy fillets
1 clove garlic
1 tbs. freshly squeezed lemon juice
1/2 cup olive oil
4 shark steaks, about 3/4-inch thick
1 tsp. garlic salt
1/2 tsp. white pepper

To make salsa verde: Place parsley, capers, anchovies, garlic, lemon juice and olive oil in a food processor workbowl or blender container. Pulse until finely chopped, but not mushy. Set aside.

Sprinkle shark with garlic salt and pepper. Place steaks in the rotisserie basket and cook for about 20 minutes, until opaque in the center.

SCALLOP KABOBS

Servings: 4

Tender scallops cook quickly, so you want to pair them up with vegetables that are best when crisp-tender.

2 red bell peppers
2 lb. sea scallops
16 white mushrooms
½ cup butter, melted
2 tbs. minced fresh chives

Peel and cut peppers into vertical quarters and cut each quarter in half for a total of 16 pieces.

Thread scallops, peppers and mushrooms onto 8 skewers. Brush melted butter over scallops and vegetables and sprinkle with chives. Place in the rotisserie and cook for about 10 to 20 minutes, depending on size of scallops, until opaque in the center.

SCALLOPS WITH HERBED BUTTER

Servings: 4

Scallops cook very quickly and should not be overcooked. They should be just opaque in the center—not firm—when they are done.

½ cup butter, melted
2 tsp. minced fresh parsley
2 tsp. minced fresh tarragon
2 tsp., minced fresh chives
½ tsp. grated lemon zest
1 lb. sea scallops

In a small bowl, combine butter, herbs and lemon zest. Thread scallops onto skewers and brush with herb butter mixture, reserving about half of the butter to serve with scallops once cooked. Place in the rotisserie and cook for about 10 to 20 minutes, depending on size of scallops, until opaque in the center. Remove scallops from rotisserie and place on a serving tray; drizzle remaining herb butter over skewers.

SHARK WITH GREEK OLIVE BUTTER

Servings: 4

A softened, flavored butter is served on top of the hot fish.

½ cup butter, softened
¼ cup minced, pitted kalamata olives
1 tbs. minced fresh chives
1 tbs. minced fresh parsley
4 shark steaks, about 6–8 oz. each
1 tsp. salt
1 tsp. white pepper

    In a small bowl, combine butter, olives, chives and parsley. Mix well. Cover and set aside while you prepare fish.
    Sprinkle salt and pepper on fish. Place in the rotisserie basket. Cook for about 20 minutes, until opaque in the center.
    To serve, place shark steaks on a serving platter and scoop about 2 tbs. of the butter onto each steak. Serve immediately.

SOFT-SHELL CRABS WITH LEMON CREAM SAUCE

Servings: 4

Although this sounds very fancy, it is a fast and easy entrée to make.

8 soft-shell crabs, rinsed and cleaned
¼ cup butter, melted
2 tbs. butter
2 tbs. flour

1 cup half-and-half
grated zest of 2 lemons
½ tsp. salt

Brush crabs with melted butter and place in the rotisserie basket. Cook for about 20 minutes, until crabs are bright red and firm. While they are cooking, prepare sauce.

Melt 2 tbs. butter in a medium saucepan over medium-low heat. Stir in flour and mix until smooth. Remove from heat. Using a wire whisk, add half-and-half slowly, stirring constantly. Return to the stove and cook until mixture reaches a thick consistency, stirring constantly. Remove from heat, stir in lemon zest and salt and serve with cooked crabs.

SPICY CATFISH

Servings: 4

This is spicy, but not overly hot.

2 tsp. olive oil
4 catfish fillets, about 6 oz. each
1 tsp. garlic salt
½ tsp. cayenne pepper
½ tsp. ground cumin

Rub olive oil on catfish. In a small bowl, mix together garlic salt, cayenne pepper and cumin. Sprinkle mixture on fish and place in the rotisserie basket. Cook for about 15 minutes, until opaque in the center.

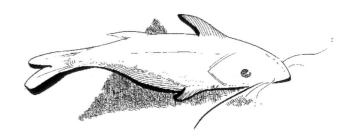

SWORDFISH WITH ROSEMARY BUTTER

Servings: 4

Even devoted meat eaters will love the taste and texture of this swordfish.

1/4 cup olive oil
4 swordfish steaks, about 6 oz. each
1/2 tsp. garlic salt
2 tbs. minced fresh rosemary, divided
1/2 cup butter
juice of 1 lemon (about 1/4 cup)
2 tbs. white wine

Rub olive oil onto swordfish. Sprinkle garlic salt on fish and pat 1 tbs. of the rosemary over fish. Place in the rotisserie basket. Cook for about 20 minutes, until fish is opaque in the center. While swordfish is cooking, prepare sauce.

In a small saucepan, melt butter over low heat. When melted, add lemon juice, white wine and remaining 1 tbs. rosemary. Keep warm over low heat.

To serve, place swordfish on a serving platter and drizzle with rosemary butter sauce.

TARRAGON TUNA

Servings: 4

Tarragon is one of my favorite herbs to use with seafood. You can also use dried dill in this recipe in place of tarragon.

2 tbs. freshly squeezed lemon juice
1 tsp. dried tarragon
¼ tsp. salt
2 tbs. olive oil
4 tuna steaks, about ½-inch thick

In a small bowl, combine lemon juice, tarragon, salt and olive oil. Rub mixture on both sides of tuna steaks. Place in the rotisserie basket and cook for about 20 minutes, until fish is opaque in the center.

TUNA WITH SAKE

Servings: 4

The Asian flavors of the sake basting sauce work well with most firm fish. This sauce can also be used on poultry.

¼ cup butter
½ cup sake
1 clove garlic, minced
1 tbs. soy sauce
1 green onion, thinly sliced
4 tuna steaks, about ½-inch thick

In a small saucepan, melt butter over medium heat. Remove from heat and add sake, garlic, soy sauce and green onion. Stir to mix.

Place tuna in the rotisserie basket and baste with sake sauce. Cook for about 20 minutes, until fish is opaque. Baste frequently with sake sauce while cooking. Discard any remaining sauce.

TEQUILA SHRIMP

Servings: 6

You can serve these as appetizers also. This recipe will serve 6 as an entrée, or 10 to 12 as an appetizer.

2 lb. large shrimp, peeled and deveined
¼ cup tequila
grated zest of 2 limes
2 cloves garlic, minced
¼ cup olive oil

Combine all ingredients in a large bowl. Toss to mix evenly. Cover and refrigerate for 1 to 2 hours.

Remove shrimp from marinade and place in the rotisserie basket. Cook for about 15 to 20 minutes, depending on size, until shrimp are pink.

TERIYAKI SALMON

Servings: 4

I never thought that the tastes of teriyaki and salmon were compatible, until I tried some at a Japanese restaurant. This teriyaki has lots of fresh ginger and pineapple juice to make a sweeter, lighter glaze than is usual with teriyaki.

1/4 cup soy sauce
1/4 cup pineapple juice
2 tbs. brown sugar, packed
1 1/2 tsp. grated fresh ginger
4 salmon steaks, about 6 oz. each

In a small bowl, combine soy sauce, pineapple juice, brown sugar and ginger. Stir until sugar dissolves.

Place salmon steaks in the rotisserie basket. Brush with teriyaki sauce and place in oven. Basting frequently with teriyaki sauce, cook for about 20 minutes, until opaque in the center. Discard any remaining sauce.

TUNA WITH LEMON BUTTER

Servings: 4

This treatment works well with fresh salmon also.

¼ cup olive oil
4 tuna steaks, about 8 oz. each
¾ tsp. garlic salt
½ cup butter
grated zest of 1 lemon
juice of 1 lemon (about ¼ cup)
2 tbs. minced fresh parsley

Rub olive oil on tuna and sprinkle with garlic salt. Place fish in the rotisserie basket and cook for about 20 minutes, until opaque in the center. While tuna is cooking, prepare butter.

In a small saucepan, melt butter over low heat. When melted, add lemon zest and juice. Keep warm while tuna cooks.

To serve, add minced parsley to lemon butter. Place tuna on a serving platter and drizzle with lemon butter.

ROTISSERIE VEGETABLES AND FRUITS

120   Easy, Flavorful Vegetables and Fruit
121   Red Potato Skewers
122   Garlic Fries
123   Curried Potatoes
124   Fiery Steak Fries
125   Rosemary Mustard Potatoes
126   Cinnamon Sweet Potatoes
127   Endive With Bacon
128   Greek Bell Peppers
129   Zucchini With Lemon Oil
130   Eggplant Roma
131   Rancher's Vegetable Skewers
132   Mediterranean Vegetables
133   Pesto Mushrooms
134   Artichoke Roast

135	Rotisserie Asparagus
136	Chinese Yard-Long Beans
137	Glazed Carrots
138	Rotisserie Celery
139	Grilled Scallions
140	Sesame Green Beans
141	Tuscan-Style Leeks
142	Deviled Potatoes
143	Root Vegetable Medley
144	Rotisserie Beets
145	Rotisserie Tomatoes
146	Sweet Rum Bananas
147	Red Wine Pears
148	Minted Pineapple
149	Apples With Blue Cheese
150	Spiced Figs

EASY, FLAVORFUL VEGETABLES AND FRUIT

The rotisserie isn't the first method of cooking vegetables that usually comes to mind. But with just a little seasoning, you can use the rotisserie to have a side dish that needs no further embellishment. The flavors of vegetables really come out more when cooked in a rotisserie than when boiled or steamed, also.

If you have multiple types of baskets with your rotisserie, I would suggest using the flat style of basket, rather than a large "tumbling" basket. The tumbling basket will work for firm vegetables like green beans or eggplant, but it will break apart other vegetables like potatoes or cauliflower.

I like to make fruit desserts in the rotisserie because I can start the cooking just as the meal begins and the dessert will be ready as we finish. The fruit recipes can be used either as desserts by themselves, or topped with ice cream, or even served on top of firm cakes such as pound cakes. They can also be served as side dishes to your entrée. Please note—you'll always want to choose ripe, but firm, fruits for these recipes, because the heat will cause any fruit to soften slightly and you don't want the end result to be mushy or broken up.

RED POTATO SKEWERS

Servings: 4–6

You'll want to buy uniformly sized potatoes, preferably about 1½ inches in diameter. These are also sold as "creamers."

2 lb. new red potatoes
¼ cup olive oil
1 tbs. minced fresh rosemary, or 1 tsp. dried, crumbled
1 tsp. garlic salt

Scrub potatoes and boil for about 7 to 10 minutes, until almost tender. Drain potatoes. When cool enough to handle, thread potatoes on skewers. Brush with olive oil and sprinkle with rosemary and garlic salt.

Place skewers in the rotisserie and cook for about 20 to 30 minutes, until fork-tender. Serve hot or at room temperature.

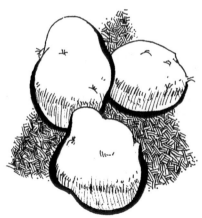

GARLIC FRIES

Servings: 4–6

These garlicky fries will disappear fast!

2 cloves garlic, minced
6 tbs. vegetable oil
6 large russet potatoes
¾ tsp. garlic salt

In a small bowl, combine garlic and oil. Let stand for 15 minutes. Cut potatoes into ½-inch strips. Toss potatoes with garlic oil and place in the rotisserie basket. Sprinkle garlic salt over potatoes and cook for about 30 to 45 minutes, until done.

CURRIED POTATOES

Most people have tasted curry when used in a main dish, but I like the way curry complements potatoes. Try this recipe with cauliflower also. Cut the head of cauliflower into florets and toss with curry mixture.

1 tbs. ground cumin
1 tbs. ground coriander
1 tsp. ground ginger
4 tsp. ground turmeric
½ tsp. cinnamon
½ tsp. salt
2 russet potatoes, scrubbed
3 tbs. olive oil

Combine cumin, coriander, ginger, turmeric and cinnamon in a small bowl. Cut potatoes into thick slices, about ¾ inch. Place in a bowl and add oil. Toss to coat.
Sprinkle curry mix over potatoes and place in the rotisserie basket. Set basket in oven and cook for about 30 minutes, until potatoes are done. Serve hot.

FIERY STEAK FRIES

Servings: 6–8

These hot and spicy fries go well with Mexican foods and most grilled meats and poultry. Adjust the amount of cayenne pepper to your personal preference.

4 russet potatoes, scrubbed
2 tbs. olive oil
2 tsp. garlic salt
1 tsp. cayenne pepper
1 tsp. chili powder

Cut potatoes into thick wedges, about 8 wedges per potato. Place potatoes in a bowl and add oil. Toss to coat.

In a small bowl, combine garlic salt, cayenne pepper and chili powder. Sprinkle mixture over potatoes. Place potatoes in the rotisserie basket. Set into rotisserie and cook for about 45 minutes, until potatoes are done and lightly browned. Serve hot.

ROSEMARY MUSTARD POTATOES

Servings: 6–8

The bold flavor of rosemary and grained mustard is perfect when serving a less seasoned, yet hearty entrée. Try serving this with a simple roast or chicken.

2 tbs. grained mustard
1 tbs. minced fresh rosemary
2 tbs. olive oil
¼ tsp. salt
4 russet potatoes, scrubbed

In a large bowl, mix together mustard, rosemary, olive oil and salt. Cut potatoes into thick wedges, about 8 wedges per potato. Add potatoes to mustard mixture. Toss to coat evenly.

Place potatoes in the rotisserie basket. Set into rotisserie and cook for about 45 minutes, until potatoes are done. Serve hot.

CINNAMON SWEET POTATOES

Servings: 4–6

This sweet potato recipe makes a nice change from mashed sweet potatoes.

1 tsp. cinnamon
1/4 cup granulated sugar
2 large yams or sweet potatoes
1/4 cup butter, melted

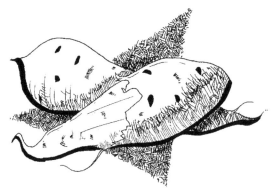

In a small bowl, combine cinnamon and sugar. Set aside. Peel and cut yams into 1 1/2-inch-thick slices. Arrange in the rotisserie basket and drizzle with melted butter. Sprinkle cinnamon-sugar over yams. Cook for about 1 hour, until tender. Serve hot.

ENDIVE WITH BACON

Servings: 4

The slightly bitter, green endive holds up well when cooked in a rotisserie. The bacon gives it a nice smoky taste.

2 slices thickly sliced bacon
4 Belgian endive heads, trimmed
freshly ground black pepper

Cook bacon in a medium skillet until crispy; remove from pan and set aside to cool. Reserve bacon fat.

Cut each endive head in half lengthwise, keeping core attached. Brush cut side with bacon fat and sprinkle lightly with pepper. Place endives in the rotisserie basket. Cook for about 45 minutes, until tender. Remove from rotisserie and place on a serving platter. Crumble cooked bacon over endives and serve hot.

GREEK BELL PEPPERS

Servings: 4–6

Serve at room temperature for a side dish, or chilled as a salad.

3 red or green bell peppers, or a combination
¼ cup olive oil, divided
1 tbs. balsamic vinegar
⅓ cup pitted kalamata olives
½ tsp. garlic salt
¼ cup crumbled feta cheese

Stem and seed peppers. Cut into quarters and lightly brush outside skins with some of the olive oil. Place peppers in the rotisserie basket and cook for about 15 minutes, until skins begin to char. Remove from basket and place in a serving bowl. Cool to room temperature.

Drizzle remaining oil over peppers and toss to coat. Add vinegar, olives and garlic salt and toss to mix well. If serving as a salad, place in the refrigerator to cool.

Just prior to serving, sprinkle crumbled feta cheese over peppers.

ZUCCHINI WITH LEMON OIL

Servings: 6

Zucchini has always been a favorite to grill or barbecue, because it holds its shape well. The rotisserie coats the zucchini with flavor.

6 medium zucchini, trimmed and halved lengthwise
$1/4$ cup olive oil
juice of 2 fresh lemons (about $1/3$ cup)
grated zest of 1 lemon
1 clove garlic, minced
$1/2$ tsp. salt

Place zucchini halves in the rotisserie basket.
In a small bowl, combine remaining ingredients and stir to mix well. Brush oil mixture over zucchini. Set aside remaining oil for basting. Cook for about 15 minutes, until zucchini are crisp-tender, basting frequently with remaining oil-lemon mixture. Serve hot.

EGGPLANT ROMA

Servings: 4–6

Serve this with your favorite pasta entrée for a stylish meal.

1 medium eggplant
1/3 cup olive oil
1 clove garlic, minced
1/2 tsp. dried oregano
1/4 tsp. dried marjoram
1/2 tsp. salt

Wash and trim eggplant. Cut into 3/4-inch-thick slices, discarding end slices. Combine oil, garlic, oregano, marjoram and salt in a small bowl and stir to mix. Brush all surfaces of eggplant with oil mixture. Place slices in the rotisserie basket. Cook for about 1 hour, until tender and lightly browned. Serve hot.

RANCHER'S VEGETABLE SKEWERS

Servings: 6

Here, ranch dressing mix is used as a base to season the vegetables.

6 thick chunks yellow crookneck squash, about 1 inch
6 large cherry tomatoes
6 large white mushrooms
6 pieces celery, about 1 inch
6 thick chunks zucchini squash, about 1 inch
1 pkg. (1 oz.) ranch dressing mix
¾ cup vegetable oil
½ cup vinegar

Thread 6 skewers with one each of the vegetables. In a medium bowl, combine ranch dressing mix, oil and vinegar together until smooth. Brush dressing over vegetable skewers. Place skewers in the rotisserie and cook for about 15 minutes, until vegetables are crisp-tender.

MEDITERRANEAN VEGETABLES

Servings: 4

The beautiful colors of this side dish will complement any entrée.

2 cloves garlic, minced
1/4 cup olive oil
1/4 tsp. dried basil
1/4 tsp. dried oregano
1/2 tsp. salt
2 zucchini, cut into 1/2-inch rounds
1/2 yellow onion, cut into 1/2-inch slices
1 red bell pepper, cut into 1/2-inch strips
1/2 small head cauliflower, broken into 1-inch florets

In a small bowl, combine garlic, oil, basil, oregano and salt. Stir to mix and let stand for 10 minutes. Place cut vegetables in the rotisserie basket and drizzle with garlic oil. Cook for about 15 to 20 minutes, until vegetables are crisp-tender.

PESTO MUSHROOMS

Servings: 4

Buy the largest white button mushrooms you can find for this recipe.

16 large white button mushrooms
¼ cup olive oil
¼ cup commercially prepared pesto
¼ cup grated Parmesan cheese

Remove stems from mushrooms and discard. In a small bowl, mix together olive oil and pesto. Add mushrooms and toss to coat well. Arrange mushrooms in the rotisserie basket and place in the oven. Cook for about 8 to 10 minutes, until tender but still firm.

Transfer mushrooms to a serving plate. Sprinkle with Parmesan cheese and serve hot.

ARTICHOKE ROAST

Servings: 4

Most people prepare artichokes by steaming or boiling them. Cooking artichokes in the rotisserie with lemon-scented oil gives them a great deal of flavor, and doesn't add as many calories as traditional mayonnaise or other dipping sauces.

¼ cup olive oil
grated zest of 1 lemon
2 whole artichokes

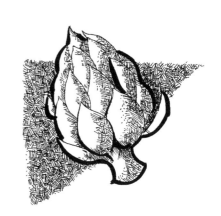

Mix together olive oil and lemon; set aside. Cut whole artichokes in half and place in the rotisserie basket, cut-side up. Drizzle olive oil and lemon zest over halves. Cook for about 1 hour, or until heart is tender when tested with a fork. Serve hot.

ROTISSERIE ASPARAGUS

Servings: 4–6

Roasting brings out a deeper asparagus flavor: no butter or added seasoning is needed.

1 lb. fresh asparagus, trimmed
2 tbs. olive oil
½ tsp. salt

Place asparagus in the rotisserie basket. Drizzle olive oil over spears and sprinkle with salt. Cook to desired doneness, about 15 minutes for crisp-tender. Serve hot.

CHINESE YARD-LONG BEANS

Servings: 4

You can find these long green beans in most supermarkets, usually near other fresh green beans. If you can't find yard long beans, this recipe works just as well with fresh green beans, or with yellow (wax) beans. It makes a great side dish with most Asian foods—not just Chinese foods.

1 tbs. sesame oil
1 tbs. olive oil
1 tbs. minced fresh garlic
1/2 tsp. red pepper flakes
1 tbs. sugar
1 tbs. soy sauce
1 lb. Chinese yard-long green beans, ends trimmed

In a large bowl, mix together sesame oil, olive oil, garlic, red pepper flakes, sugar and soy sauce. Stir until sugar has dissolved. Add beans and toss to coat.

Place green beans in the rotisserie basket. Set basket in the rotisserie and cook for about 15 to 20 minutes, until beans are crisp-tender. Remove from basket and set on a serving platter. Serve hot.

GLAZED CARROTS

Servings: 4–6

The naturally sweet carrots get a brown sugar glaze in this super-easy recipe.

1 lb. carrots
2 tbs. butter, melted
2 tbs. brown sugar, packed

Cut carrots into 1-inch chunks. Place in the rotisserie basket. Drizzle melted butter over carrot chunks and sprinkle with brown sugar. Cook to desired doneness, about 30 minutes for crisp-tender. Serve hot.

ROTISSERIE CELERY

Servings: 4

Plain, everyday celery stalks turn into an amazing side vegetable when cooked in the rotisserie oven.

12 stalks celery, trimmed
1/4 cup olive oil
2 tsp. celery salt
1/2 tsp. freshly ground black pepper

Arrange celery stalks in the rotisserie basket. Drizzle with olive oil and sprinkle with celery salt and pepper. Cook for about 20 minutes, until crisp-tender. Serve hot.

GRILLED SCALLIONS

Servings: 4

You may think this is a strange recipe, but if you like grilled onions with your meats or poultry, try these green onions for a change.

16 scallions, trimmed
¼ cup olive oil
1 clove garlic, minced
½ tsp. garlic salt
½ tsp. freshly ground black pepper

Arrange onions in the rotisserie basket. In a small bowl, mix together oil, garlic, salt and pepper. Drizzle olive oil mixture over scallions. Cook for about 15 minutes, until crisp-tender. Serve hot.

SESAME GREEN BEANS

Servings: 4

This Asian-flavored dish can be spiced up if you use hot sesame oil instead of regular toasted oil.

1 lb. green beans, ends trimmed
2 tbs. sesame oil
½ tsp. salt
1 tbs. sesame seeds

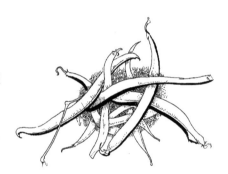

Place green beans in the rotisserie basket and drizzle with sesame oil. Sprinkle with salt. Cook for about 20 minutes, until beans are crisp-tender. Remove from basket to a serving platter. Sprinkle with sesame seeds. Serve hot.

TUSCAN-STYLE LEEKS

Serves 4

You'll use only half of the marinade while cooking the leeks. The rest will be used as a vinaigrette dressing. These are best served at room temperature.

4 medium leeks
1 cup olive oil
1 clove garlic, minced
1 tbs. dried oregano

1/4 cup balsamic vinegar
2 tbs. white wine
1/2 cup chopped fresh tomatoes

Cut leeks in half lengthwise. Trim bottoms and trim leeks to fit in your rotisserie basket. Place all leeks cut-side up in basket.

In a small bowl, mix together olive oil, garlic, oregano, balsamic vinegar and white wine. Pour 1/2 of the mixture over cut side of leeks. Marinate for 15 minutes.

Place basket in oven and cook until tender, about 30 minutes. Remove from basket to a serving platter. Drizzle remaining vinaigrette over leeks and scatter chopped tomatoes over.

DEVILED POTATOES

Serves 4–6

Red-tinted and fiery hot, these potatoes make a great side dish for grilled entrées.

1 tbs. red pepper flakes
1 tbs. paprika
1 tbs. chili powder
6 tbs. vegetable oil
6 large russet potatoes
1/2 tsp. garlic salt

In a small bowl, combine red pepper flakes, paprika, chili powder and oil. Cut potatoes into 1-inch wedges. Toss pepper oil with potatoes and let stand for 15 minutes. Place potatoes in the rotisserie basket. Sprinkle garlic salt over potatoes, and place basket in rotisserie. Cook for about 45 minutes, until done.

ROOT VEGETABLE MEDLEY

Serves 4

These vegetables are available year-round, but I think the tastes and colors are perfect for autumn.

2 turnips, peeled and cut into 1/2-inch-thick slices
2 carrots, cut into 2-inch pieces
2 parsnips, peeled and cut into 1/2-inch-thick slices
2 tbs. olive oil
2 tbs. honey
2 tbs. orange juice

Arrange vegetables in the rotisserie basket. In a small bowl, mix together oil, honey and orange juice. Drizzle over vegetables.

Place in the oven, and cook for about 60 to 80 minutes, until the vegetables are tender.

ROTISSERIE BEETS

Serves 4–6

Fresh beets taste so much better than any canned product. Here, they are cooked with a touch of herbs to accent their sweetness. Add these to a baby spinach salad for a beautiful salad of deep green and red.

1 lb. fresh beets
2 tbs. olive oil
1 tbs. fresh lemon juice
½ tsp. fresh minced tarragon

Trim ends and leaves from beets, and peel. Cut into ½-inch-thick slices. Arrange in the rotisserie basket.

Mix together oil, lemon juice and tarragon. Drizzle over beets. Place basket in rotisserie, and cook for 35 to 45 minutes, or until tender. Serve warm or at room temperature.

ROTISSERIE TOMATOES

Serves 6–8

Using seeded tomatoes will give you a side dish with intense tomato flavor, much more than a traditional baked or stuffed tomato.

4 beefsteak tomatoes
¼ cup olive oil
2 tbs. white wine
2 tbs. tarragon vinegar

Cut tomatoes in half horizontally. Gently remove seeds from halves. Place tomatoes cut-side down on paper towels to help absorb as much liquid as possible. Let stand for 20 minutes.

Place tomatoes in the rotisserie basket. In a small bowl, combine olive oil, wine, and vinegar. Drizzle over tomato halves. Place basket in the oven and bake for 45 minutes.

SWEET RUM BANANAS

Servings: 6

The bananas get a beautiful dark glaze as they cook; try serving this with rum raisin ice cream. Be sure to use ripe, but firm bananas for this, or you'll get a mushy result.

6 firm bananas
¼ cup rum
¼ cup dark brown sugar, packed
1 tsp. lemon juice

Peel bananas and place whole in the rotisserie basket. Combine rum, brown sugar and lemon juice and brush over bananas. Cook for about 25 minutes, until bananas are tender and glazed. Baste frequently with remaining glaze. Serve hot.

RED WINE PEARS

Servings: 4

If you have ever had poached pears, you know how wine complements this fruit. You can cook the pears while you have your dinner, so your dessert will be ready right afterwards.

2 cups red wine
¾ cup sugar
½ tsp. cinnamon
2 large, firm, ripe Bosc pears

In a medium saucepan, mix together wine, sugar and cinnamon and bring to a boil over high heat. Stir frequently until sugar dissolves. Pour wine mixture into a shallow dish.
Cut each pear in half and core. Place each half, cut-side down, in warm wine mixture. Marinate for 2 hours.
Place pear halves in the rotisserie basket and discard marinade. Cook for about 30 minutes, until tender. Serve hot.

MINTED PINEAPPLE

Servings: 4–6

Pineapple is one of my favorites for the rotisserie oven; cooking it in the rotisserie keeps it much juicier than cooking it on the grill.

1 large, ripe pineapple, peeled, cored and cut into 8 wedges
¼ cup butter, melted
¼ cup chopped fresh mint
¼ cup sugar

Arrange pineapple in the rotisserie basket and drizzle with melted butter. Sprinkle mint over pineapple. Cook for about 20 minutes, until hot and juicy. Remove from basket and place on a serving platter. Sprinkle sugar over wedges. Serve hot.

APPLES WITH BLUE CHEESE

Servings: 4

This can be served as an appetizer, a side dish or as part of a cheese or dessert course.

2 Granny Smith apples
1/4 cup butter, melted
1/2 cup crumbled blue cheese
1/4 cup chopped walnuts

Cut apples in half and core. Brush cut sides with butter and place in the rotisserie basket. Cook for about 15 to 20 minutes, until apples are beginning to soften, but are not mushy.

Arrange each apple half on a serving plate, cut-side up. Place 2 tbs. blue cheese in the cavity of each apple. Sprinkle 1 tbs. chopped walnuts over each apple and serve while warm.

SPICED FIGS

Serves 4

Fresh figs become a delicacy when lightly spiced and cooked. Allow 2 figs per person when preparing.

8 fresh figs, cut in half
2 tbs. sugar
1/4 tsp. nutmeg
1/4 tsp. ground ginger

Place figs in the rotisserie basket, cut-side up. In a small bowl, combine sugar, nutmeg and ginger. Sprinkle mixture over cut figs. Place basket in the oven and cook figs for about 15 minutes.

Remove to a serving plate. If desired, serve with a scoop of rich vanilla ice cream.

INDEX

A

Apples with blue cheese 149
Apricot-glazed chicken 73
Artichoke roast 134
Asparagus, rotisserie 135
Avocado salsa with salmon 104

B

Bacon chicken, smoky 80
Bacon with endive 127
Baja marinade for seafood 14
Bananas, sweet rum 146
Basil lemon chicken 36
Beans, Chinese yard-long 136
Beef
    cooking large cuts of 59
    cooking small cuts of 31
    herbed sirloin roast 60
    Jack Daniel's roast 61
    Korean skewers 56
    pepper-crusted T-bones 57
    prime rib with horseradish sauce 63
    ranch rub for 13
    red wine marinade for 26
    rib eye roast with Madeira 62
    sate skewers 52
    steaks with sherried mushrooms 54
    Tuscan marinade for 27
    western bbq burgers 51
Beets, rotisserie 144
Bell peppers, Greek 128
Bell peppers, red, with lamb chops 43
Blue cheese with apples 149
Bourbon and peaches with pork chops 48
Bourbon orange hens 88
Buffalo wings, better than 32
Burgers, lamb 44
Burgers, western bbq 51
Butter
    Greek olive, with shark 109
    herbed, with scallops 108
    lemon, with tuna 117
    rosemary, with swordfish 112

C

Cajun snapper 93
Carrots, glazed 137
Catfish, spicy 111
Celery, rotisserie 138
Cheese, blue with apples 149
Chicken (see also Poultry)
    apricot-glazed 73
    breasts, rosemary 34
    country herbed 74
    cumin skewers 37
    glistening kung pao 38
    hot honey 76
    lemon basil 36
    lemon lime 75
    Moroccan stuffed 78
    orange teriyaki 39
    pineapple 35
    sesame skewers with dipping sauce 33
    smoky bacon 80
    super spicy 81
Chili-seasoned salmon 94
Chinese bbq pork ribs 46
Chinese yard-long beans 136
Chives with red snapper 103
Cinnamon sweet potatoes 126
Citrus marinade for seafood 18
Couscous, in Moroccan stuffed chicken 78
Crabs, soft-shell, with lemon cream sauce 110
Cranberries with pork loin 67
Creole rub 8
Cuban pork loin 66
Cumin chicken skewers 37
Curried potatoes 123
Curry game hens with kiwi salsa 84

D
Deviled potatoes 142
Dijon marinade for poultry and seafood 19
Dijon tuna steaks 95
Dill with salmon 105
Dipping sauce with sesame chicken skewers 33
Dried rubs and marinades 3-29

E
Eggplant Roma 130
Endive with bacon 127

F
Figs, spiced 150
Fish: see Seafood
Fries, fiery steak 124
Fries, garlic 122
Fruit
    apples with blue cheese 149
    cooking methods 120
    minted pineapple 148
    red wine pears 147
    spiced figs 150
    sweet rum bananas 146

G
Game hens, honey and ginger 87
Game hens, orange bourbon 88
Garlic fries 122
Garlic scampi 96
Ginger and honey game hens 87

Ginger orange marinade for pork or poultry 25
Greek bell peppers 128
Green beans, sesame 140
Green onions with trout 100

H
Halibut, Provence 102
Halibut with spicy salsa 97
Herb
    marinade for poultry, fresh 20
    marinade for seafood 15
    rotisserie turkey, fresh 82
    rub for lamb 10
Herbed
    butter with scallops 108
    country chicken 74
    sirloin roast 60
    turkey burgers 40
Herbes de Provence 6
Herbs with pork 69
Honey and ginger game hens 87
Horseradish sauce with prime rib 63
Hot honey chicken 76

I
Instant-read thermometers, about 2
Italian beef rub 9
Italian marinade for poultry 22

J
Jack Daniel's roast 61

Jamaican jerk rub for pork or poultry 11
Jamaican pork chops 47

K
Kabobs (see also Skewers)
    scallop 107
    spring lamb shish 41
    scallop 107
Korean beef skewers 56
Kung pao chicken, glistening 38

L
Lamb
    burgers 44
    chops with red peppers 43
    mint marinade for 23
    rosemary leg of 70
    sage rub for 12
    shish kabobs, spring 41
    tarragon kabobs 42
Leeks, Tuscan-style 141
Lemon
    basil chicken 36
    butter with tuna 117
    lime chicken 75
    oil with zucchini 129
Lime lemon chicken 75

M
Madeira, with rib eye roast 62
Maple mustard turkey breasts 86

Maple-glazed pork loin 65
Marinades
    Baja, for seafood 14
    citrus, for seafood 18
    Dijon, for poultry and seafood 19
    fresh herb, for poultry 20
    herb, for seafood 15
    Italian, for poultry 22
    mint, for lamb 23
    orange ginger, for pork or poultry 25
    for pork 24
    red wine, for beef 26
    for seafood 16
    tarragon, for seafood 17
    Tuscan beef 27
    whisky, for ribs 28
    white wine, for poultry 21
Marinating seafood 5
Mediterranean vegetables 132
Mint marinade for lamb 23
Minted pineapple 148
Mixed seafood skewers 98
Moroccan stuffed chicken 78
Mushrooms, pesto 133
Mushrooms, sherried with steaks 54
Mustard maple turkey breasts 86
Mustard pork roast 64
Mustard rosemary potatoes 125

O

Old Bay rub for seafood 7

Orange
    bourbon hens 88
    ginger marinade for pork or poultry 25
    teriyaki chicken 39

P

Pacific Rim trout 99
Peaches and bourbon with pork chops 48
Pears, in red wine 147
Pepper-crusted T-bones 57
Pesto mushrooms 133
Pineapple chicken 35
Pineapple, minted 148
Pork
    Chinese bbq ribs 46
    chops with bourbon and peaches 48
    chops with citrus salsa 49
    chops, Jamaican 47
    cooking large cuts of 59
    cooking small cuts of 31
    endive with bacon 127
    with herbs 69
    Jamaican jerk rub for 11
    loin with cranberries 67
    loin, Cuban 66
    loin, maple-glazed 65
    marinade for 24
    mustard roast 64
    orange ginger marinade for 25
    roast with sage 68

Potatoes
    curried 123
    deviled 142
    red, on skewers 121
    rosemary mustard 125
Poultry
    apricot-glazed chicken 73
    buffalo wings, better than 32
    cooking small cuts of 31
    cooking whole 72
    country herbed chicken 74
    cumin chicken skewers 37
    curry game hens with kiwi salsa 84
    Dijon marinade for 19
    fresh herb marinade for 20
    fresh herb rotisserie turkey 82
    ginger and honey game hens 87
    glistening kung pao chicken 38
    herbed turkey burgers 40
    hot honey chicken 76
    Italian marinade for 22
    Jamaican jerk rub for 11
    lemon basil chicken 36
    lemon lime chicken 75
    Moroccan stuffed chicken 78
    mustard maple turkey breasts 86
    orange ginger marinade for 25
    orange teriyaki chicken 39
    pineapple chicken 35
    rosemary chicken breasts 34
    sage rub for 12

Poultry, *continued*
   sesame chicken skewers with dipping sauce 33
   smoky bacon chicken 80
   super spicy chicken 81
   white wine marinade for 21
   whole 71-89
Prawn skewers with prosciutto 101
Prime rib with horseradish sauce 63
Prosciutto prawn skewers 101
Provence halibut 102

R
Ranch rub for beef 13
Red potato skewers 121
Red snapper with chives 103
Red wine marinade for beef 26
Red wine pears 147
Ribs, whisky marinade for 28
Roasts
   herbed sirloin 60
   Jack Daniel's 61
   mustard pork 64
   pork with sage 68
   rib eye with Madeira 62
Root vegetable medley 143
Rosemary
   butter with swordfish 112
   chicken breasts 34
   leg of lamb 70
   mustard potatoes 125
Rotisserie oven cooking, about 1

Rubs
   Creole 8
   herb, for lamb 10
   herbes de Provence 6
   Italian beef 9
   Jamaican jerk, for pork or poultry 11
   Old Bay, for seafood 7
   ranch, for beef 13
   sage, for lamb or poultry
Rum with bananas, sweet 146

S
Sage
   with pork roast 68
   rub for lamb or poultry 12
   with veal chops 50
Sake with tuna 114
Salmon
   with avocado salsa 104
   chili-seasoned 94
   with dill 105
   teriyaki 116
Salsa
   avocado, with salmon 104
   kiwi, with curry game hens 84
   spicy with halibut 97
   verde with shark 106
   citrus, with pork chops 49
Sauce, horseradish, with prime rib 63
Sauce, lemon cream, with soft-shell crabs 110
Sausages and veggies 45

Scallions, grilled 139
Scallop kabobs 107
Scallops with herbed butter 108
Seafood
   Baja marinade for 14
   Cajun snapper 93
   chili-seasoned salmon 94
   citrus marinade for 18
   cooking methods 92
   Dijon marinade for 19
   Dijon tuna steaks 95
   garlic scampi 96
   halibut with spicy salsa 97
   herb marinade for 15
   marinade for 16
   mixed skewers 98
   Old Bay rub for 7
   Pacific Rim trout 99
   prosciutto prawn skewers 101
   Provence halibut 102
   red snapper with chives 103
   salmon with avocado salsa 104
   salmon with dill 105
   salsa verde shark 106
   scallop kabobs 107
   scallops with herbed butter 108
   shark with Greek olive butter 109
   soft-shell crabs with lemon cream sauce 110
   spicy catfish 111
   swordfish with rosemary butter 112
   tarragon marinade for 17

Seafood, *continued*
   tarragon tuna 113
   tequila shrimp 115
   teriyaki salmon 116
   trout with green onions 100
   tuna with lemon butter 117
   tuna with sake 114
Sesame chicken skewers with dipping sauce 33
Sesame green beans 140
Shark salsa verde 106
Shark with Greek olive butter 109
Shish kabobs, spring lamb 41
Shrimp, see garlic scampi 96
Shrimp with tequila 115
Skewers (see also Kabobs)
   beef sate 52
   cumin chicken 37
   Korean beef 56
   mixed seafood 98
   prosciutto prawn 101
   rancher's vegetable 131
   red potato 121
   sesame chicken 33
Smoky bacon chicken 80
Snapper, Cajun 93
Spiced figs 150
Spicy catfish 111
Spicy chicken, super 81
Spring lamb shish kabobs 41
Steak fries, fiery 124
Sweet potatoes, cinnamon 126

Swordfish with rosemary butter 112

T
T-bone steaks, pepper-crusted 57
Tarragon
   lamb kabobs 42
   marinade for seafood 17
   tuna 113
Tequila shrimp 115
Teriyaki orange chicken 39
Teriyaki salmon 116
Thermometers, instant-read. about 2
Tomatoes, rotisserie 145
Trout, Pacific Rim 99
Trout with green onions 100
Tuna
   with lemon butter 117
   with sake 114
   steaks with Dijon 95
   with tarragon 113
Turkey breasts, mustard maple 86
Turkey burgers, herbed 40
Tuscan beef marinade 27
Tuscan-style leeks 141

V
Veal chops with sage 50
Vegetables
   artichoke roast 134
   Chinese yard-long beans 136
   cinnamon sweet potatoes 126
   cooking methods 120

   curried potatoes 123
   deviled potatoes 142
   eggplant Roma 130
   endive with bacon 127
   fiery steak fries 124
   garlic fries 122
   glazed carrots 137
   Greek bell peppers 128
   grilled scallions 139
   Mediterranean 132
   pesto mushrooms 133
   rancher's skewers 131
   red potato skewers 121
   root medley 143
   rosemary mustard potatoes 125
   rotisserie asparagus 135
   rotisserie beets 144
   rotisserie celery 138
   rotisserie tomatoes 145
   sesame green beans 140
   Tuscan-style leeks 141
   zucchini with lemon oil 129

W
Whisky marinade for ribs 28
White wine marinade for poultry 21

Z
Zucchini with lemon oil 129

Serve Creative, Easy, Nutritious Meals with nitty gritty® Cookbooks

100 Dynamite Desserts
The 9 x 13 Pan Cookbook
The Barbecue Cookbook
Beer and Good Food
The Best Bagels are Made at Home
The Best Pizza is Made at Home
Bread Baking
Bread Machine Cookbook
Bread Machine Cookbook II
Bread Machine Cookbook III
Bread Machine Cookbook IV
Bread Machine Cookbook V
Bread Machine Cookbook VI
Cappuccino/Espresso
Casseroles
The Coffee Book
Convection Oven Cookery
Cooking for 1 or 2
Cooking in Clay
Cooking in Porcelain
Cooking on the Indoor Grill
Cooking with Chile Peppers
Cooking with Grains
Cooking with Your Kids

Creative Mexican Cooking
Deep Fried Indulgences
The Dehydrator Cookbook
Edible Pockets for Every Meal
Entrées From Your Bread Machine
Extra-Special Crockery Pot Recipes
Fabulous Fiber Cookery
Fondue and Hot Dips
Fresh Vegetables
From Freezer, 'Fridge and Pantry
From Your Ice Cream Maker
The Garlic Cookbook
Gourmet Gifts
Healthy Cooking on the Run
Healthy Snacks for Kids
The Juicer Book
The Juicer Book II
Lowfat American Favorites
Marinades
Muffins, Nut Breads and More
The New Blender Book
New International Fondue Cookbook
No Salt, No Sugar, No Fat
One-Dish Meals

The Pasta Machine Cookbook
Pinch of Time: Meals in Less than 30 Minutes
Recipes for the Loaf Pan
Recipes for the Pressure Cooker
Recipes for Yogurt Cheese
Risottos, Paellas, and other Rice Specialties
Rotisserie Oven Cooking
The Sandwich Maker Cookbook
The Sensational Skillet: Sautés and Stir-Fries
Slow Cooking in Crock-Pot,® Slow Cooker, Oven and Multi-Cooker
The Steamer Cookbook
The Toaster Oven Cookbook
Unbeatable Chicken Recipes
The Vegetarian Slow Cooker
The Versatile Rice Cooker
Waffles
The Well Dressed Potato
Worldwide Sourdoughs from Your Bread Machine
Wraps and Roll-Ups

For a free catalog, call: Bristol Publishing Enterprises, Inc.
(800) 346-4889
www.bristolcookbooks.com